SOPHISTICATED WEALTH MANAGEMENT
MADE SIMPLE

The SteelPeak Approach to
Financial Planning and Investing

Reza Zamani,
Maziar Esmailbeigi,
Ali Zamani

With the assistance of Rodney Brooks

All rights reserved. No part of this publication may be reproduced, distributed or transmitted in any form or by any means, including photocopying, recording, or other electronic or mechanical methods, without the prior written permission of the publisher, except in the case of brief quotations embodied in critical reviews and certain other noncommercial uses permitted by copyright law. For permission requests, contact the publisher.

SteelPeak Wealth: www.steelpeakwealth.com

SteelPeak Wealth is an independent financial planning and investment advisory firm that seeks to empower private clients with the direction and discipline to build their wealth for every life stage and their legacies for the future.

Sophisticated Wealth Management Made Simple—Reza Zamani, Maziar Esmailbeigi, Ali Zamani, 1st ed.

ISBN 9798676776145

Steel Peak Wealth Management, LLC ("SteelPeak") is an SEC registered investment adviser located in California. SteelPeak may only transact business in those states in which it is notice filed, or qualifies for an exemption or exclusion from notice filing requirements. This publication is limited to the dissemination of general information regarding SteelPeak's investment advisory services to United States residents residing in states where providing such information is not prohibited by applicable law. Accordingly, this publication should not be construed by any consumer and/or prospective client as SteelPeak's solicitation to effect, or attempt to effect transactions in securities, or the rendering of personalized investment advice for compensation. Furthermore, information in this book should not be construed, in any manner whatsoever, as the receipt of, or a substitute for, personalized individual advice from SteelPeak. Any subsequent, direct communication by SteelPeak with a prospective client shall be conducted by a representative that is either registered or qualifies for an exemption or exclusion from registration in the state where the prospective client resides.

This publication contains information derived from third party sources. Although SteelPeak believes these third party sources to be reliable, SteelPeak makes no representations as to the accuracy or completeness of any information prepared by any unaffiliated third party incorporated herein, and take no responsibility therefore.

This publication also contains certain forward-looking statements which indicate future possibilities. Due to known and unknown risks, other uncertainties and factors, actual results may differ materially from the expectations portrayed in such forward-looking statements. As such, there is no guarantee that the views and opinions expressed in this publication will come to pass.

Any hypothetical example provided in this publication is intended for illustrative purposes only and does not represent an actual client or an actual client's experience, but rather is meant to provide an example of the process and methodology. Individual client experience may vary based on individual circumstances. SteelPeak provides no assurance that it will be able to achieve similar results in comparable situations.

We are neither attorneys nor your accountants and no portion of this publication should be interpreted as legal, accounting or tax advice. We recommend seeking the advice of a qualified attorney and accountant.

This publication was prepared in collaboration with a third party author not affiliated with SteelPeak. The third-party author researched material and prepared the text. SteelPeak maintained creative and executive control over the publication's content.

For information pertaining to the registration status of SteelPeak, please refer to the SEC's web site at www.adviserinfo.sec.gov. A copy of SteelPeak's current written disclosure brochure discussing SteelPeak's business operations, services, and fees is available from SteelPeak upon written request.

This book is dedicated to our clients, who have entrusted us with managing their family wealth

Someone's sitting in the shade today
because someone planted a tree a long time ago

~Warren Buffet

Table of Contents

About Us i
    Reza Zamani, Founding Partner iii
    Maziar Esmailbeigi, Founding Partner v
    Ali Zamani, Founding Partner vii
    Our Firm: SteelPeak Wealth viii
The Six-Step Process 1
    Step 1: Determine Goals 2
    Step 2: Assess Current Investments and Risk Tolerance 3
    Step 3: Discuss Financial Plan and Investment Strategy 4
    Step 4: Implement Your Investment Strategy 5
    Step 5: Monitor and Rebalance Portfolio 6
    Step 6: Comprehensive Review and Reporting 7
Adviser vs. Broker 9
The Personal Life Plan 15
    Having a Plan Is the Most Important Step 19
    Starting a Business 20
    Volunteering 21
    Part-Time Job or Consulting 22
    Serving Your Church or Synagogue 23
    Spending More Time with the Children or Grandchildren . 24
Unexpected Retirement Costs 25
    Children, Grandchildren, and Other Family Members 25
    Grandchildren 27
    Other Family Members 28
    Starting a Business 28
    Home Repairs and Updates 30

Health Insurance 31
Health Care 32
Long-Term Care 32
Investment Strategy & Risk 35
Passive vs. Active Investment Strategy 35
Traditional vs. Non-Traditional Investments 37
Options 39
Covered Call Option Strategy 40
Cash-Secured Put Option Strategy 41
Taxable, Tax-Deferred, and Tax-Free 45
Taxable Accounts 46
Tax-Deferred Accounts 47
Tax-Free Accounts 49
Accumulation of Wealth vs. Distribution of Wealth 53
Accumulation 54
Compound Interest 55
The Rule of 72 56
Risk 56
Distribution 60
Tax Planning 63
Proper Tax Planning Is Not Seasonal 64
Stay Up-to-Date on Tax Laws 65
Mutual Funds and Capital Gains 67
Sometimes It Is Okay to Sell a Stock and Pay Taxes on the Gains 67
Estate Planning 69
Living Trust 71
Take an Active Approach to Planning 73
Living Will 74

Passing More Than Just Dollars 75
Insurance Planning 77
    Life Insurance 79
    Health Insurance & Medicare 80
    Disability Insurance 83
    Long-Term Care Insurance 84
Emotions of Investing 87
    Taxes Are Inevitable 92
    Conclusion 93
Acknowledgments 95
Contact Us 97

INTRODUCTION
About Us

Have you read the headlines about Americans and how ill-prepared they are for retirement? One survey shows 74 percent of Americans are behind in their retirement savings.[1] The Federal Reserve says 40 percent of Americans would not have enough in their savings to cover a $400 emergency.[2]

We could go on, but you get the point.

Americans are not saving enough, and, as a result, we are headed for a retirement crisis. More than ever, we need financial advice—unbiased financial advice, in particular, without the influence of specific product sales.

That's where we come in.

---

[1] Dana Larsen. A Place for Mom. April 20, 2018. "Why 74% of Americans Are Not Ready for Retirement." https://www.aplaceformom.com/blog/americans-are-not-ready-for-retirement/

[2] Federal Reserve. May 28, 2019. "Report on the Economic Well-Being of U.S. Households in 2018 - May 2019." https://www.federalreserve.gov/publications/2019-economic-well-being-of-us-households-in-2018-dealing-with-unexpected-expenses.htm

We are SteelPeak Wealth, an independent financial planning and investment advisory firm headquartered in the Los Angeles area.

We are dedicated to helping our clients achieve their most important financial goals as effectively and safely as possible. We are fiduciary wealth managers, which means we have a duty to serve your best interest and not subordinate your interest to our own.

Our comprehensive financial planning and investment solutions are customized to each client's unique goals, and our extensive expertise and resources empower clients to thrive during each stage of their lives. We pride ourselves on our independence, which enables us to provide objective advice to our clients without hidden agendas.

To start, we want to tell you a little about the individuals who make SteelPeak Wealth a quality enterprise.

Reza Zamani, Founding Partner

I, Reza, did not grow up with the proverbial silver spoon in my mouth, and I suspect most people reading this did not, either. Frankly, I was broke when I started my career. I worked two jobs during my college years and played four years of soccer for a Division I NCAA program. The scholarship I received to play soccer at the University of California at Santa Barbara paid for only part of my education in business economics, but I was grateful for even that small contribution. From the very beginning, you could say, it has been ingrained in my DNA to work smart and hard.

A UC-Santa Barbara alumnus, who worked for a major Wall Street firm, offered me an unpaid internship while I was in college. The internship required working five days a week without any pay. Since my scholarship only covered tuition, I was already working a part-time job to pay for my general expenses, on top of attending class, soccer games, and practices. But I saw an opportunity through the internship to learn more about the wealth management industry, and my two years as an unpaid intern were invaluable.

By the time I graduated, I knew I wanted to be a financial adviser. I went back to Los Angeles, where I grew up, and got licensed with a boutique firm. I worked fifteen-hour days and spent weekends meeting with potential clients and learning about the industry.

I knew the first few years would be a lot of hard work with little immediate reward, but I remembered what my parents always taught me: Delay gratification. Do not worry about rewards today. Stay disciplined. While my friends were gushing about two-week vacations and company perks, I focused on becoming the best financial adviser I could by reading as many books and publications as possible.

I had been warned financial planning and wealth management were careers for people who were already wealthy or who knew a lot of wealthy people. Call me stubborn (or optimistic), but I did not believe that then, and I surely do not believe it now.

In the early part of my career, I held monthly educational seminars teaching investors about comprehensive financial planning. Realizing the big brokerage firms were only focusing on asset management, I saw an opportunity to join a larger firm (PaineWebber) and bring the element of holistic planning to the industry. This was fortuitous, due to the timing of the downturn of the equity markets in 2000 to 2001, which presented an opportunity for new advisers like me to teach existing investors a new way to focus on wealth.

I stayed at Paine Webber (which was later acquired by UBS) for eight years. Due to my sports background and belief in the team concept, I focused on creating a "financial team" to work with clients, in order to provide holistic, comprehensive service.

This led to partnering with Maziar Esmailbeigi and Ali Zamani. The concept of teamwork is important to me; each member should provide a different element of skill while sharing the same vision and philosophy. Thus, the three of us became partners with the shared vision of creating a disciplined financial process and the shared philosophy of always putting the client first. Our team left UBS and joined Morgan Stanley. After five years of working with high net worth clients, we started SteelPeak Wealth to move into a new chapter of being fiduciary advisers.

Maziar Esmailbeigi, Founding Partner

I am Maziar, and I lived the American dream. Well, not exactly. As a child of immigrants, I witnessed the long hours my parents worked in our small family business to provide for my brother and me. By my teenage years, I was working after school and on weekends right alongside my parents. My father spoke very broken English, often asking me to take on business conversation on his behalf, and, in turn, I learned quickly about business, investing, and saving. I grew up in Lake Tahoe, Nevada, and attended the University of Nevada. I then moved to Los Angeles and graduated from Cal State University at Northridge with a major in biology. Obviously, I didn't know I would end up in finance. So, how did that happen?

You see, I am the black sheep of my family. Most of my relatives are either physicians or dentists. I did not want to disappoint my parents, so I majored in biology, with the intention of attending dental school. However, in college I found a passion for investing. I was investing for myself and my family, and I began to wonder if I could have a career in finance.

Initially, what attracted me to the financial industry was stock trading. Of course, that is not what we do for clients today. It was an entirely different world when I started in the business. Back then, stockbrokers would telephone people, recommend they buy a stock, and charge them a large commission, which is much different from today.

When I decided to pursue my passion for finance, I reached out to UBS PaineWebber. That's where I met Reza, who, at the time, was screening potential advisers for the firm. That's when we started to formulate our shared vision of creating a plan to provide clients with a different method of wealth management. Then, Ali Zamani joined us a few years later, and we created an even stronger partnership by focusing on each of our strengths.

We moved from UBS to Morgan Stanley in 2008, and, after five years, decided to form SteelPeak Wealth as a way to challenge the industry status quo and use our talents to serve our clients as fiduciary advisers.

Each of us has a different role to play. My entrepreneurial background helps give me a sense of the challenges business owners face. I am very good at being a psychiatrist and helping our clients understand investing, which is essential for all of our goals in serving our clients.

The concept of being a part of a team is important, and, as Reza says, each of us brings a different skillset to the table. But we all still share the same vision and philosophy.

Ali Zamani, Founding Partner

My childhood memories of witnessing the hard work of my parents paved the road for my mindset in life. I went to the University of California at Santa Barbara where I earned a degree in business economics.

While I was in school, I took an internship with Smith Barney in Santa Barbara. I learned a lot about the business and realized it was my passion.

When I graduated, the industry was still recovering from the market correction of 2001. Most financial services firms were not hiring. So, instead, I went into the insurance industry. It was a great experience—learning how to interact with people and focus on wealth transfer using sophisticated insurance strategies.

A few years later, I joined Reza and Maziar at UBS Wealth. At this point in my career, I learned the importance of working in a team environment to help clients reach their financial goals. Through training, I learned more about the areas of the business I was passionate about and gained the skills I could add to our team. We moved from UBS to Morgan Stanley, and after a few years we realized we could move into an independent space and, as SteelPeak Wealth, could offer our clients a fiduciary advisory service. The vision we created early on in our partnership is still the foundation of what we are accomplishing for our clients today.

I have a passion for this business. I enjoy interacting with people and helping them reach the goals we develop together at SteelPeak Wealth. I also enjoy creating unique strategies to help them reach those financial goals.

I love what we can achieve together as a team. We know our clients have worked hard for their wealth, and they put a lot of trust in our firm. It is our responsibility to maintain that trust with our diligent work and dedicated service.

Our Firm: SteelPeak Wealth

In 2012, after a combined thirty years of industry experience with major Wall Street firms, we launched SteelPeak Wealth. The vision of the firm is "Sophisticated Wealth Management Made Simple," reflected in the title of this book.

Following, we will walk through, at a high level, our process and the ideas that drive it.

Chapter 1: The Six-Step Process

We have come to embrace this process after watching many investment fads come and go. At SteelPeak Wealth, we put every potential new client through our six-step process, one that continues throughout their lifetimes.

Chapter 2: Adviser vs. Broker

What separates a true wealth adviser from a broker boils down to the fiduciary rule.

This rule underpins fiduciary duty and represents the legal requirement for financial advisers to work in their customers' best interest.

Chapter 3: The Personal Life Plan

One part of retiring is financial. The other part, which Americans tend to underestimate, relates to your lifestyle in retirement. What will you do when you no longer have that nine-to-five job to go to?

Chapter 4: Unexpected Costs in Retirement

Now is a good time to talk about unexpected costs that could complicate or even ruin your retirement. If you have been diligent about sitting down to form a retirement plan with your financial adviser, you won't be surprised by unexpected costs.

Chapter 5: Investment Strategy & Risk

Our first step for new clients is to create a personalized financial plan. Once we review and approve that plan, we establish an investment strategy to delineate your specific investment goals and objectives and pair them with carefully selected investment strategies.

Chapter 6: Taxable, Tax-Deferred, and Tax-Free

There are three distinct ways to set aside money—taxable accounts, tax-deferred accounts, and tax-free accounts. Money in taxable accounts is good, money in tax-deferred accounts is better, and money in tax-free accounts is the best.

Chapter 7: Accumulation of Wealth vs. Distribution of Wealth

These two stages require completely different strategies and philosophies. Even if a client makes it through the first phase without a financial adviser, it is highly advisable to seek financial help when it comes to replacing their weekly, or bi-weekly, paycheck with withdrawals from retirement accounts.

Chapter 8: Tax Planning

When it comes to taxes, there is tax planning, and there is tax preparation. It's important you understand the difference.

Chapter 9: Estate Planning

Estate planning is more about rewarding the next generation. It concerns the legacy you want to leave behind. The benefits of this type of planning are less for you as a client and more for your beneficiaries.

Chapter 10: Insurance Planning

The most popular components of financial planning include asset and debt management, but another important part of caring for the needs of our clients is insurance. When it comes to wealth management, we look at insurance to protect our clients from the loss of income, to protect them from the risk of estate taxes, or to protect them from high expenses associated with long-term care.

Chapter 11: Emotions of Investing

Investment decisions can be highly emotional. This can lead to some truly terrible financial decisions.

We hope as you read you consider how these principles might make a difference in a sound financial planning process, and that the thoughts and concepts we outline will give you questions and new ideas about how to implement your own sophisticated, yet simple, wealth management plan. Thank you for reading.

CHAPTER 1
The Six-Step Process

Let's talk about process—how to approach growing, protecting, and using your assets. Process is different than strategy, which can be defined as the general direction or route you choose to reach your goals. Process is a well-thought-out series of steps you take to construct the road to financial security. It helps keep you disciplined.

We have come to embrace this concept of following a process after watching many investment fads come and go. At SteelPeak Wealth, the products and strategies will vary from person to person, but the process will stay the same. We put every potential new client through our unique six-step process, and that process never ends. As you'll see as you read further in this chapter, we believe strongly in process over product at SteelPeak Wealth.

The idea of following a process is not unlike building a house. Each house will ultimately end up looking very different, but the teams responsible for building them will follow the same process of laying a foundation, planning HVAC, plumbing, and electrical, etc. Each team member (the plumber, electrician, carpenter) may have a specialty, but it takes them all following the process together to have a well-constructed house.

It's the same way with constructing a financial plan. You want something that suits your interests and needs, but something that follows a process or checklist, a repeatable set of steps that ensure all the pieces get taken care of. Through our careers, we have developed a process based on the commonalities we saw from helping hundreds of people retire over the years, which is what we use to drive our planning at SteelPeak.

Here is how it works:

Step 1: Determine Goals

What We Do: We will help you identify your goals by dividing them into needs, wants, and wishes. You can manage finances better during retirement if you have a good understanding of how many expenses should fall into each category. Once you figure that out, you can assign funds to provide for each goal in the most efficient way.

How It Benefits You: By building your unique outline, we will form the foundation for a productive partnership focused on identifying each of your goals, as well as discovering where they fall in order of priority for you. We don't have any cookie-cutter plans; by beginning with your specific dreams and needs, your plan will be based on a foundation that is unique to you—this is what we believe everyone we work with needs and deserves.

Summary: Our first meeting with a new client is very similar to a job interview. There is a lot we want to know about both you and your family. This stage in the process is also when we begin our data gathering. We'll ask you to bring all relevant information and paperwork, including your most recent tax returns, brokerage and bank statements, insurance policies, and your monthly budget.

Step 2: Assess Current Investments and Risk Tolerance

What We Do: We will analyze your existing investment allocation and cash flow. We will also determine your personal risk profile. A risk profile is an evaluation of your willingness and ability to take risks. It is necessary for determining a proper asset allocation for your portfolio.

How It Benefits You: We will determine the projected growth and cash flow of your current investments to determine how much of your portfolio depends on capital appreciation (i.e., how much your finances depend on the market rising or some circumstance that raises the value of your assets) versus income. We will then determine your risk tolerance to find the appropriate balance between potential rewards and potential risks included in your plan. This is partly about what your finances can realistically handle, and partly about finding your emotional comfort zone. Having a plan that frankly and openly works with your risk in mind can help keep you from making knee-jerk or emotional decisions in times of market turmoil.

Summary: After the first meeting, we will begin to analyze the information you provided in order to formulate an outline of your current investment strategy and risk.

Step 3: Discuss Financial Plan and Investment Strategy

What We Do: We will show you the probability of success for your financial plan, along with a complete stress-test analysis. We will then present our investment strategies for you using our proprietary research, with an emphasis on helping you control and build your personal cash flow.

How It Benefits You: By understanding your goals and risk, we can discover different opportunities and personalize a strategy to best suit your personal situation. Stress testing your portfolio can give you an idea of what your financial picture might look like in different scenarios and help you strengthen any areas of weakness. Above all, we hope that by showing how your portfolio acts in different scenarios—think market drops, personal health events, hyperinflation—we can give you confidence in your plan's long-term durability.

Summary: We review the goal-based comprehensive plan. We prioritize your goals and put them in one of three buckets—Needs, Wants, or Wishes. Needs are the essentials, such as housing, utilities, food, basic clothing, and health care. You generally want to pay for them from your reliable income sources. Wants are things like a new wardrobe, entertainment, or hobbies and sports like golf or tennis. You should be able to cover your wants with earnings from your distributions. Wishes include that trip around the world, a new car, a diamond ring, or that beach house you've been dreaming about for years. We suggest taking profits from your investments to cover the costs of your wishes. In good times, you will buy more of your wishes. During periods of short-term uncertainty, you may not buy as many luxury items as during the good times.

We then show you your current allocation, risk, assets, liabilities, percentage of each goal funded, and your overall probability of success.

After we present you with the financial plan, we move toward an investment strategy, which we recommended based on your specific goals. Our investment philosophy is to focus on cash flow within our investment strategies. There are two ways you make money: Selling assets that have appreciated or having assets that generate a cash flow. Some clients will have both. Regardless, how you make money is crucial when approaching investment strategies. We're strong believers in focusing on this.

Step 4: Implement Your Investment Strategy

What We Do: We will work with our Institute of Portfolio Management & Economic Strategy (this is our personal, SteelPeak Wealth-specific committee that monitors and researches the quality of investment strategies) to implement your plan. We take taxes and market conditions into consideration during this phase while adhering to the guidelines of the financial plan.

How It Benefits You: Your financial plan will establish a clear understanding of investment goals and objectives, leading to the effective long-term implementation of your portfolio.

Summary: This is the step where we begin implementing the investment strategy we have discussed with you. At this stage, your investments are transferred to us for management. This phase could take anywhere from a few weeks to a few months— the timeline will be based on the best scenario for tax implications and market conditions. One of the best ways to manage market risk is to invest using a dollar-cost averaging method of investing periodically over time to factor in the ups and downs of the markets.

Step 5: Monitor and Rebalance Portfolio

What We Do: Your portfolio will be proactively managed by our Institute of Portfolio Management & Economic Strategy, along with the oversight of your wealth management team.

How It Benefits You: Once we implement your plan, your dedicated wealth management team and the Institute of Portfolio Management & Economic Strategy continuously monitor your portfolio to ensure your investments continue to meet the strict criteria set forth in your written investment policy. This makes sure that, if one investment really excels or another frankly doesn't, we can keep you from being overexposed or out of balance in any one area, and be sure to continually keep you in line with your written plan.

Summary: We actively manage the portfolio while taking into consideration the client's existing goals and objectives, and the current market conditions. The financial plan will always serve as the foundation for the goals, and the written investment policy will be the blueprint to monitor the risk.

Step 6: Comprehensive Review and Reporting

What We Do: Your wealth management team will provide you with a quarterly performance report and a comprehensive semi-annual.

How It Benefits You: Communication between you and your wealth management team at SteelPeak Wealth will drive any adjustments to your financial plan and investment strategy. After all, your goals and needs may change over time, and this ongoing dialogue gives you an avenue to be sure your investments are always in line with your life circumstances.

Summary: We return to your original financial plan and re-ask many of those interview questions. We mostly ask about what has changed in your life. Are there any health issues we need to be aware of? Have your expenses changed? Do you have any new goals? Are you retiring sooner?

Our vision of how to best help clients has evolved into something more than just numbers. It's about our clients' lives. It is qualitative as well as quantitative, and it includes flexibility, which is where Step 6 comes in. Anything from the date of retirement to the birth of a grandchild or death of a spouse can radically alter your goals and the means to achieve them. That is why a regular review of the plan is a must.

We've been fortunate to know and work with many people who could be called "comfortably well-off" or even "rich," to use the old term. But following the process has helped many more clients *create* wealth. It's the concept we've come to embrace after seeing many investment trends rise and fall.

CHAPTER 2

Adviser vs. Broker

In the last chapter, we talked about our process. In our first meeting with a client, we make it clear who we are and what we do. Our firm is registered with the U.S. Securities and Exchange Commission (SEC) as a registered investment adviser to provide investment advisory and financial planning services in accordance with fiduciary standards.

Many other advisers operate under a dually registered structure. This means they can operate as a broker *or* as an investment adviser. We believe this is a flaw in the system. To be a true fiduciary, you should not have the option to do anything outside of being a fiduciary. When you are dually registered, that presents a problem. We believe if you can take your fiduciary hat off and put on a broker hat, you are a broker, period.

What's the best way to know if your adviser is a fiduciary? An investment adviser is required to have a Form ADV, which you can either ask the adviser to present directly or search for online under the SEC or state regulators' websites.[3] Also, any adviser who is registered with the SEC as an investment adviser is held to the fiduciary standard of operating in your, the client's, best interests. Any investor looking to work with a wealth adviser should ask, point blank, if an adviser is a fiduciary prior to accepting a meeting. The second question to ask is whether the wealth adviser is dually registered. If their answer is yes, you should be aware their ability to act as a fiduciary is compromised.[4] If they answer "no," you should feel comfortable enough with the standard of care they owe you to proceed.

These days, just about anyone can call themselves a financial adviser or wealth adviser, regardless of their registration status.

What separates a true wealth adviser from a broker comes down to the fiduciary standard of care.

A fiduciary standard obligates the standard bearer, in this case the investment adviser, to disclose any conflicts of interest and to only make recommendations that are in the best interest of the consumer—not putting their own financial desires ahead of the needs of the client.

In other words, you will not have to worry about a fiduciary trying to sell you products just so they can receive a commission. A true adviser is a fiduciary. Every decision he or she makes is for the benefit of the clients. This ranges from decisions about investments and investment strategy all the way to the selection of the custodian who will hold the funds. An

---

[3] Michael F. Kay. *Forbes.* May 14, 2019. "How Do You Know If Your Financial Advisor Is Acting In Your Best Interests?"
https://www.forbes.com/sites/michaelkay/2019/05/14/how-do-you-know-if-your-financial-advisor-is-acting-in-your-best-interests/#4817a06a14e4
[4] Ibid.

investment adviser owes you a fiduciary duty to put your interests first for every part of the process and over the course of your entire advisory relationship.

Fiduciary financial advisers are looking at all aspects of a client's concerns and ensuring the client's interests are always first.

Ultimately, one difference between investment advisers and brokers is the broker has a heightened responsibility to their parent firm. This means he or she must prioritize assets or investments that benefit the company as well as attain "suitability" for the client. Do you see how that compromises his or her loyalty to the client a bit? You can sit with two different financial planners, and both can have the same title of wealth adviser. The difference requires you to peel away the onion. Under it you must look at how they are operating. Are they operating under an independent platform where they can use a wide range of products, or are they operating under the rules of a bank, brokerage firm, or insurance company? The average person sees the business card and thinks they are the same, but now you know how to tell the difference.

The actions we take and services we provide as fiduciary advisers are driven by what brings value to our clients. There cannot be any hidden fees, additional incentives, or anything that results in us benefiting from what we are doing without fully disclosing the situation to our clients. A broker can and *will* be compensated for what particular investment recommendations they use, and he or she does not have to fully disclose what compensation they receive for their services as an adviser or for a product they recommend to the client.

Two words separate the two: fiduciary responsibility. The basic definition of fiduciary responsibility is the legal obligation to act in the best interest of a client. The question, now, is: Do you know whether or not your adviser is a fiduciary? A 2019 Financial Trust survey showed 48 percent of Americans believe *all* financial advisers have a distinct obligation to act in the best interests of their clients.[5] Unfortunately, as we've just elaborated, this is not the case. Be sure that when you are ready to seek professional advice, you are getting independent, conflict-free advice from a fiduciary.

After you determine if your adviser is a fiduciary, there are many other considerations to make to help you judge and determine which financial adviser is the one for you. While you want to be as thorough as possible, the process does not need to be difficult. Do you simply want help choosing and managing investments? Or, do you have a more complicated financial situation that goes beyond investment needs? Considering these questions can help you focus your search for the right financial adviser.

It's also important to understand how much these services will cost before you commit to a firm. Investment advisers often charge a percentage of the total asset amount they manage, with a median fee of 1 percent, although it can range higher for small accounts and lower for large ones. Others may charge a flat fee, an hourly rate, or a retainer.

You should always check out the record of the company or person you're considering. Look up the firm's Form ADV, the key disclosure document investment advisers must file with the U.S. Securities and Exchange Commission and state securities authorities. Among other things, this form will outline how the

---

[5] Carlos Dias, Jr. *Kiplinger.* June 3, 2019. "7 Secrets Financial Advisers Won't Tell You." https://www.kiplinger.com/article/retirement/T023-C032-S014-7-secrets-financial-advisers-won-t-tell-you.html

firm or adviser charges for its service (and what the specific fees are), what conflicts of interest they may have, and any past disciplinary actions enacted against them.

Common questions you should ask before you hire a financial adviser include:

- **Are you a fiduciary?** We've devoted most of the chapter to this.

- **What are the fees and how do you get paid?** Advisers can use a variety of fee structures, such as percentage of the assets under management, a flat fee, or an hourly fee. You should be aware of other fees, which can decimate your savings over time. A NerdWallet analysis found a 1 percent mutual-fund fee could cost millennials $590,000 in retirement savings over time.[6] Be aware of hidden fees in mutual funds.

- **How much access will you have?** Talk to the adviser about how often you'll meet and how available they are for phone calls and emails. You want to know you will have access to your adviser if you have questions or concerns, especially during a volatile market stretch.

- **What is your investment philosophy?** You need to know whether how your money is invested agrees with your personal investment philosophy. If you are a careful or conservative investor, you don't want to have someone investing your savings aggressively. You may want to also

---

[6] Dayana Yochim and Jonathan Todd. NerdWallet. "How a 1% Fee Could Cost Millennials $590,000 in Retirement Savings."
https://www.nerdwallet.com/blog/investing/millennial-retirement-fees-one-percent-half-million-savings-impact/

ask about their clients. The adviser who worked for your father may not be the best one for you.

- **Do you have a custodian?** In the best of all worlds, your financial adviser would cultivate a relationship with an independent custodian who would actually manage your investment. Ideally, an independent custodian, such as a brokerage companies like Charles Schwab & Co, Inc. and Fidelity, or another company not affiliated directly to your adviser, would be responsible for holding your investments. Remember, Bernie Madoff, who defrauded clients through a multibillion-dollar Ponzi scheme, acted as his own custodian. The independent custodian can act as an important safety check.

Interviewing advisers is a crucial part of the process. Through these questions, you will be able to determine if that adviser is a good fit for you. You must be comfortable and not feel this person is talking down to you or over your head. And it's not out of the question to interview three, or more, advisers—much like you would before hiring a contractor to do work in your home.

CHAPTER 3
The Personal Life Plan

People generally think of planning for retirement as a financial issue. The truth is, it is much more than just a financial plan. Many people have retired with plenty of savings, but they have still struggled emotionally. Why is that? Well, only part of retiring is financial. The other part, which many Americans tend to underestimate, has to do with your lifestyle in retirement.[7] What will you do when you no longer have that nine-to-five job to go to? What will your reason be for getting out of bed each morning?

Just how difficult is retirement for some people? For many people, especially men, their job is their identity. Retirement is especially difficult for them, as they report more boredom, anxiety, restlessness, and feelings of uselessness. The Centers for Disease Control and Prevention reported retired

---

[7] Jonathan Burton. MarketWatch. August 4, 2019. "You're probably not ready to retire — psychologically." https://www.marketwatch.com/story/why-youre-probably-not-psychologically-ready-to-retire-2019-05-21

men were 40 percent more likely than employed men to experience depression.[8]

That is why a personal life plan is much more than income, expenses, and investment returns. Part of your plan includes looking at the qualitative part of life. What is important to you and your family? What will your legacy be? What do you want to accomplish in life?

As people lead longer and healthier lives, a person retiring from full-time work at the age of sixty-five today will likely live another twenty, or even thirty, years.[9]

Though most of this book is an attempt to encourage you to think about how you'll save, invest, and spend your money, the point of this chapter is to make you think about how you will spend your time. At SteelPeak Wealth, we believe the two are equally important.

As much as you might look forward to retirement, it can be an extremely jolting experience. Those of us who do not replace it with something else can experience a significant personal crisis trying to regain a sense of value. Even if they are financially able to retire, many people are not psychologically prepared for the endeavor.

According to another study, women tend to dream about retirement, viewing it as a time to pursue their new goals and

---

[8] Ibid.
[9] Kathleen Coxwell. NewRetirement. February 19, 2020. "The 12 Best Life Expectancy Calculators and Why You Should Use One When Planning Your Retirement." https://www.newretirement.com/retirement/longevity-trends-and-life-expectancy-calculators/

find meaningful work in other areas of their life. This includes volunteering with local charities and joining social groups.[10]

Men tend to tie their self-worth to their job or occupation, and they are more likely to have a difficult time adjusting when they are no longer identified as a lawyer or an engineer.[11] [12]

The point is, retirement certainly can be something to look forward to, but it can be an extremely unsettling experience as well.

So, regarding your retirement plan, we recommend planning for more than just the numbers. Make sure to have a road map that includes your lifestyle plans after retirement and is flexible and open to change.

Ask yourself questions like:

- Where do you want to live during your retirement? Will you "age in place," move to a retirement community, or buy a dream retirement home in a warm-weather state like Florida or Arizona?

- Do you want to be close to your children or grandchildren? Will that require you to pull up stakes and move?

---

[10] Catherine Collinson, Patti Rowey, and Heidi Cho. TransAmerica Center for Retirement Studies. November 14, 2019. "19 Facts About Women's Retirement Outlook." https://www.transamericacenter.org/docs/default-source/women-and-retirement/tcrs2019_sr_women_and_retirement_research_report.pdf
[11] Donna McCaw. Retire Happy. January 12, 2020. "Issues that men face in retirement." https://retirehappy.ca/issues-that-men-face-in-retirement/
[12] Matteo Picchio and Jan van Ours. Vox. February 2, 2020. "How retirement can affect mental health: Lessons from the Netherlands." https://voxeu.org/article/how-retirement-can-affect-mental-health

- Do you plan to travel once you retire? For most people, travel increases in the first decade or so of retirement and tapers off as they age.

- What do you plan to do in retirement? Do you have hobbies that might take up your time?

- What kind of retirement lifestyle do you envision?

- Do you plan to get more involved at your church or a nonprofit?

The answers to these questions will determine how we allocate your funds. It provides a list of things important to you at this stage in your life. All of them are important to put into a financial plan to help guide us as we try to meet your objectives. As you tell us your goals, some may require financing. For those, we will figure out how to fund them, from which financial sources you can fund them, or if you can fund them at all.

Seventy percent of Americans say they want to travel in retirement.[13] In fact, it's the most common retirement dream. But travel can be costly.

So, our question for clients is what kind of travel are you planning? Are we talking about travel three or four times a year to visit the kids or grandkids? That's fairly easy to budget for, but even that cost can spiral—especially if you're talking about a coast-to-coast flight or a flight to a smaller or out-of-the way city.

---

[13] Rebecca Lake. Investopedia. November 1, 2019. "How to Plan for Travel in Retirement." https://www.investopedia.com/retirement/how-plan-travel-retirement/

Or, are you planning to take that once-in-a-lifetime trip to Europe, or that Mediterranean cruise you and your spouse have been dreaming of since you got married? Are you planning to take a big international trip every year or every other year?

This goes back to the first chapter where we talked about needs, wants, and wishes. The key is that we must write your dreams about travel into your financial plan so we can factor it into your budget.

Also, keep in mind most people cut back considerably on their travel once they reach their eighties. Any goals related to travel expenses should take into consideration the client's age in retirement. For example, a husband and wife who retire at age seventy might travel more throughout their seventies, but it's likely that expense will decrease significantly in their eighties. Again, it is all about flexibility with your goals and periodic adjustments to your plan.

Having a Plan Is the Most Important Step

The last thing you want to do is wake up at 6 a.m. on your first Monday after retirement and have nothing to do. It won't take you long to be bored out of your mind. You will need a reason to get up in the morning, and watching sports on TV all the time may not be the healthiest lifestyle to choose during retirement.

Plan out your day and your week. Have activities planned. If you are married to someone who is already retired or has been at home for a while, they may not necessarily want you to jump into their activities. Have your own time and activities planned.

Hobbies are important. This is your time. For some, it's simple things like gardening. But, for others, it could be learning a new language, writing a book, creating a podcast, creating art, etc. The list goes on. Do something you love or that you have always wanted to do.

Here are some examples. Two ladies in New England started writing mystery novels with baby boomers as the main characters. Art sites frequently feature pieces by people in their second careers who found out how to turn their long-time hobbies into income.

And then there's golf or other sporting activities. The biggest mistake some people make with golf is they plan to play every day, and, eventually, they get bored. Have multiple activities and people in your life so you are not dependent on just one thing. It's not just with your money where the "all your eggs in one basket" maxim holds true.

Some smart golf junkies have landed part-time jobs at their local golf resorts. Not only does this give them something to do, but they can also reduce expenses with the discounts on their games and equipment.

Starting a Business

Increasingly, retirees are refusing to ride off into the sunset. Many are retiring from their corporate jobs only to become entrepreneurs—and they are doing it at record rates.[14] It can be a viable option, but, first, it must be in your financial plan.

According to one survey, the number of Americans who continue to work after age sixty-five has doubled since 1985.[15] Another survey says 65 percent of Americans polled said they dream of opening a business when they reach retirement.[16] You can read more about this in the next chapter.

Volunteering

Now, understand we don't have to write *everything* into your financial plan. We just want to do our job to make sure you live out a happy retirement and don't run out of money.

Many people plan to spend more time volunteering at their church or at a non-profit in their community in retirement. Some retirees even say they are busier in retirement than they were when they had full-time jobs.

We can help you with this important part, even if it means simply talking it out. You need to have a plan to do something with your time when you no longer must respond to that alarm

---

[14] John Timpane. *AARP*. November 15, 2019. "More Adults Over 50 Starting Their Own Businesses." https://www.aarp.org/work/small-business/info-2019/older-adults-becoming-entrepreneurs.html
[15] John F. Wasik. *Forbes*. June 3, 2019. "Why Working Past Retirement Age May Make Sense." https://www.forbes.com/sites/johnwasik/2019/06/03/why-working-past-retirement-age-may-make-sense/#5c4a71afa799
[16] Atomik Research. The UPS Store. March 20, 2019. "Inside Small Business: Second Annual Survey Reveals Entrepreneurial Spirit Remains Strong." https://www.theupsstore.com/insidesmallbusiness

at 6 a.m. every day. As the old adage says, "Those who fail to plan are planning to fail." It's something many people forget.

Remember, you probably spent years on the job with colleagues you will no longer see every day. Many people closely connect their identities with their occupations, and this transition to a new lifestyle can have an emotional impact.

Volunteering may not be in your plans when you retire, but we encourage our clients to think about things they want to do in retirement. This is not your grandfather's retirement where people could kick back in their easy chairs and watch TV westerns.

According to one study, the people happiest in retirement are those who have decided "giving back" and discovering a sense of purpose is important to them.[17]

All in all, that personal life plan can be just as important as that financial plan.

Part-Time Job or Consulting

There's no doubt about it, people are living longer, and, thus, they are working longer. So, while some people are ready to retire from the jobs they are working on, they are not necessarily ready to stop working completely.

---

[17] ESI Money. February 26, 2020. "How to Have a Happy Retirement." https://esimoney.com/how-to-have-a-happy-retirement/

According to the U.S. Bureau of Labor Statistics, more than half of people aged sixty to sixty-four work, and a third of people aged sixty-five to sixty-nine worked at least part time in 2017.[18]

Most experts suggest that, if you want to keep working, the best bet is to see if you can continue working part-time or as a consultant for your current employer. But some pre-retirees want to do something completely different.

Whether it's work at Home Depot or in the golf shop at your local golf course, retirees are working to keep busy and make sure they have something to do.

Serving Your Church or Synagogue

There are boundless opportunities to volunteer at your church or synagogue. Some retirees find they spend so much time working with their religious organizations that they are busier than they were when they were working. Talk with your local religious leaders about how you could best help, and ask if there are needs that might play to your strengths. With countless committees, this is one place you are certain to find plenty to do.

---

[18] Carl Hunnel. Richland Source. April 30, 2019. "More older Americans remaining in the workforce—or trying to return."
https://www.richlandsource.com/gray_matters/more-older-americans-remaining-in-the-workforce---/article_8c41aa72-6a83-11e9-9da9-0f84e30a3439.html

Spending More Time with the Children or Grandchildren

For some people, the most important thing to use time on in retirement is to spend more time with family—especially children and grandchildren. If they don't live nearby, it might mean more travel.

If you will be visiting three or four times a year, it's best to build those expenses into your travel budget, especially if you will be flying. If there's an annual trip to Disneyland or Disneyworld, the costs can quickly spin out of control between transportation, hotel, and park entry fees.

But, like many of these activities, babysitting and visiting can get old for some people. Make sure you have other things planned to break up your routine.

CHAPTER 4
Unexpected Retirement Costs

Sometimes hobbies have unexpected costs. Remember, unless you own a golf course, it's not free to play golf every day. And, for some people, there is a thin line between a hobby and a business. Make sure you know the difference.

This is a good time to talk about unexpected costs that can complicate, or even ruin, your retirement. You won't be surprised by unexpected costs if you have been diligent about sitting down with your financial adviser and getting that retirement plan done.

Children, Grandchildren, and Other Family Members

People will do virtually anything for their children. Parents will sacrifice much to keep their children happy. They will send them to private schools they can't afford or even buy expensive clothes and tech gadgets. And then there's college tuition. It's not uncommon for some parents to raid their retirement accounts to pay college tuition.

The point is, children can be expensive. That also doesn't change much when they leave home. Thus, there are certain expenses that must be included in your financial plan. That, of course, includes college tuition. It's also not uncommon for some high school students to take a year off before going to college and travel through Europe. If you're paying for that, like many parents do, it's causing the effect of paying five years of college tuition rather than four. This is why it's important to plan and budget.

Then there's the part when kids come back home. Children moving back home after college, after a divorce, or when they just need help paying their monthly expenses are all very real scenarios, and they are all budget busters.

We know cases in which retired parents were paying for cell phones, car payments, and even rent for their grown children—sometimes even when they couldn't afford it.

One study found millennials were the least likely of any generation before to own a home, and they were more likely to live with someone, sometimes without contributing to the cost of housing (such as living with parents).[19]

We're not saying you shouldn't help your children when they need you. But having your son or daughter moving back home

---

[19] Jung Choi. New America. "Homeownership and Living Arrangements among Millennials: New Sources of Wealth Inequality and What to Do about It." https://www.newamerica.org/millennials/reports/emerging-millennial-wealth-gap/homeownership-and-living-arrangements-among-millennials-new-sources-of-wealth-inequality-and-what-to-do-about-it/

with two children after a break-up can be an expensive proposition for a retiree, especially if they are not paying for or sharing expenses. Boundaries, deadlines, and finances need to be discussed, and your financial adviser should help update your financial plan when an unexpected circumstance like this arises. If your resources are stretched to the limit, don't hesitate to let your financial adviser be the heavy hand in your discussion with your children.

Grandchildren

One AARP report estimated grandparents spend about $179 billion a year on their grandchildren, an average of $2,562 a year.[20] That doesn't sound like a lot and, as far as we're concerned, that estimate is probably too low. AARP says some grandparents, though, were spending much more for their grandchildren's education costs alone. The report also said:[21]

- 21 percent, about 14.7 million, spent an average of $4,075 annually

- 7 percent had taken on debt to help their grandchildren pay for college, and 1.23 million had incurred credit card debt or co-signed private student loans

Again, as with children, retirees need to be careful they do not spend money in a way that will cause them unnecessary

---

[20] *AARP.* 2019. "2018 Grandparents Today National Survey: Money and the Modern Grandparent Fact Sheet."
https://www.aarp.org/content/dam/aarp/research/surveys_statistics/life-leisure/2019/aarp-grandparenting-study-money-fact-sheet.doi.10.26419-2Fres.00289.017.pdf
[21] Ibid.

hardship. One financial adviser told a story of a grandmother who repeatedly ignored his advice and continued to send money to her grandson. He advised against it because she didn't really have the money to spare. We can't tell you how this story ends because, by the time he told the story, she had completely spent down her retirement account and was, therefore, no longer his client.

Other Family Members

Everybody has at least one in the family. It could be a brother, a cousin, an uncle, or a niece. They are always facing an eviction or some other crisis and need a loan. Again, we won't tell you not to help your family. Our advice is simply not to help a family member when it would put your retirement in danger. Again, if you need help saying no, set up a meeting, and let us be the bad guys.

Starting a Business

Increasingly, retirees are refusing to relegate themselves to a rocking chair or porch swing. Instead, they are using retirement as the opportunity to start a second or even third act as entrepreneurs, turning hobbies into careers like they always dreamed. [22]

If that's something you hope to do, great. But please, plan ahead and build that into your financial picture.

---

[22] John Timpane. *AARP*. November 15, 2019. "More Adults Over 50 Starting Their Own Businesses." https://www.aarp.org/work/small-business/info-2019/older-adults-becoming-entrepreneurs.html

Let's say you love to bake. You want to turn that love of baking into a hobby selling cupcakes. Remember our discussion of needs, wants, and wishes? We would drag the cupcake business over into the "want" column.

Then, we would start asking you questions. What do you want to accomplish? Are you looking to keep it at a hobby level and sell cupcakes out of your kitchen to friends, relatives, and former co-workers who know you can make an excellent cupcake? Or, do you want to rent a store and work with your spouse and family? Will you need staff?

Your capital requirements will depend on the answers to all those questions. But, first, we need to point out the certain dangers to funding your new business out of your retirement savings, especially if it's the money you will live on.

Let's start with some statistics:[23]

- 20 percent of new businesses fail in year one
- 33 percent fail in year two
- 50 percent fail in year five

We don't want to discourage you from your lifelong dream. But, keep in mind, insufficient capital and poor planning are the two leading reasons for business failures. So, if you know the risks and want to proceed, you need to make sure you have the resources to withstand the possible loss of your funds. Plus, you need to have a strong business plan. Your financial adviser, your

---

[23] G. Dautovic. Fortunly. July 17, 2019. "Examining What Percentage of Small Businesses Fail." https://fortunly.com/blog/what-percentage-of-small-businesses-fail/#gref

accountant, and your lawyer should all be involved in such an endeavor.

Now, if you feel confident and want to proceed, you need to make sure your financial adviser is intricately involved in your financial plans. Say, hypothetically, you will need $50,000 to be ready to become an entrepreneur when you retire in 2022. We'll then put that goal in the plan and figure out where the money will come from.

How much are your projected profits? Do we need to look at funding it from your current income so we don't have to touch your retirement income? Here's a big question: How will funding this business affect your taxes and your lifestyle?

Sometimes that dream is not a real option. There are times when we have to sit down with a client and make them face the hard facts. Suppose you need $100,000 in start-up costs, but you only have $500,000 in your retirement account. In that case, we will have to resort to plan B or plan C.

If the bank won't lend you the money because you don't have experience, what about an equity line of credit? We go through all the options by listing the pros and cons so, together, we can make an intelligent decision.

Home Repairs and Updates

Despite all those stories about the best places to retire, the vast majority of people retire in the same homes they've lived in—usually where they raised their families. So, before you retire (and while you're still working) we'd suggest you make sure you pay attention to upkeep, so you don't get hit unexpectedly with big-ticket repairs after retirement.

Some of the biggest costs, no matter where you live in the United States, are probably replacing the roof and replacing the HVAC systems. According to homeadvisor.com, replacing a roof in 2020 generally costs somewhere in the range of $5,349 to $10,686, or an average of $7,915.[24] Replacing an HVAC system can vary widely, depending on the brand and the installation costs, but a $3,777 to $7,427 estimate should be in the ballpark for most homeowners.[25]

Health Insurance

One big mistake we hear about often is people who retire before age sixty-five and forget, if they are no longer in that corporate job, they have to go out on the open market and find health insurance on their own. It can be prohibitively expensive.

It's easy to forget, since your company has been bearing the brunt of those health insurance payments for years. If your spouse is not retired and can add you to his or her policy, no problem. Otherwise, you will need to find your own health insurance.

Of course, when you reach age sixty-five, you become eligible for Medicare. But, make sure you apply during the proper window and follow all the rules. A mistake could increase your premiums for life.

---

[24] Dan DiClerico. April 16, 2020. HomeAdvisor. "How Much Does It Cost to Replace or Install A Roof?" https://www.homeadvisor.com/cost/roofing/install-a-roof/
[25] Dan DiClerico. April 16, 2020. HomeAdvisor. "How Much Does It Cost to Install Central Air?" https://www.homeadvisor.com/cost/heating-and-cooling/install-an-ac-unit/

Health Care

According to one study, a sixty-five-year old couple retiring this year can expect to spend $285,000 on health care and medical expenses throughout retirement. For unmarried retirees, the estimate is $150,000 for women and $135,000 for men.[26]

Medical debt, in fact, is one of the main reasons for the fast-increasing bankruptcy rate among seniors and retirees. In fact, a study by the National Council on Aging showed medical debt as one of the most significant obstacles keeping older citizens from economic well-being.[27]

Long-Term Care

Someone turning sixty-five today has about a 70 percent chance of needing some type of long-term care.[28] Sometimes a client will ask us to plan for if they ever need assisted living or long-term care arrangements. This then creates another area where we need to make provisions and set aside funds.

Long-term care expenses are generally needed for three to four years, and those costs can eat into a significant portion of one's

---

[26] Fidelity. April 2, 2019. "Health Care Price Check: A Couple Retiring Today Needs an Estimated $285,000 as Medical Expenses in Retirement Remain Relatively Steady." https://www.fidelity.com/bin-public/060_www_fidelity_com/documents/press-release/healthcare-price-check-040219.pdf
[27] National Council on Aging. 2018. "Senior Debt Facts."
https://www.ncoa.org/economic-security/money-management/debt/senior-debt-facts/
[28] Moll Law Group. 2019. "The Cost of Long-Term Care."
https://www.molllawgroup.com/the-cost-of-long-term-care.html

retirement assets.[29] In certain cases, proper planning requires the use of long-term care insurance as needed.

---

[29] Ibid.

CHAPTER 5
Investment Strategy & Risk

As we said earlier, our first step for new clients is to create a personalized financial plan. Once we review and approve that plan, we establish an investment policy. This investment policy would delineate your specific investment goals and objectives and pair them with carefully-selected investment strategies.

Your personal investment policy statement also details your risk and return objectives, your asset allocation, your recommendations for specific investments, and any tax considerations you may have.

Our commitment to a financial-planning-based approach grows from a dedication to our clients' overall well-being. Our goal is to help you identify and achieve your goals and, ultimately, help you live a more secure and fulfilling life.

Passive vs. Active Investment Strategy

Investment strategy boils down to whether money is managed actively or passively.

Passive investing, used by many financial advisers, seeks to maximize returns by minimizing buying and selling. Index investing is one common example of a passive investing strategy. Using this strategy, investors purchase an asset based on a benchmark, such as the S&P 500 index. Another of these passive investing strategies includes the purchase of mutual funds. Both employ a buy-and-hold method of investing.

At SteelPeak Wealth, we believe in an active strategy of investing, which involves using individual securities, exchange-traded funds, and alternative investments, with active rebalancing.

There is a strong connection between market performance and the economy's continual cycle of expansion and contraction. As market conditions change, we make adjustments with the aim of taking advantage of opportunities and minimizing risk. The goal is to improve return without taking on significant additional risk.

We harness the power of the market to help our clients meet their distinct goals. To achieve this, we use a broad range of investment strategies to tailor portfolios to each client's unique objectives, time horizon, and comfort level of risk. At the heart of our approach is the bedrock investing principle called the *"Efficient Frontier."*

Introduced in 1952 by Nobel Prize-winning economist Harry Markowitz, the Efficient Frontier principle is the very best framework available for maximizing returns for a given level of risk in a portfolio. Its principles guide us in how we select the basic mix of asset types within your portfolio. These assets may include stocks, bonds, and cash, but one way we differ from many other financial advisers is we try to optimize your results by incorporating alternative investments.

We custom design a strategy for each client based on their individual needs and situation. Based on that, we design a strategy and create a custom solution. We determine what exposure our clients should have to traditional investments (stocks and bonds) and what exposure they should have to non-traditional investments.

Traditional vs. Non-Traditional Investments

We don't need to spend much time explaining traditional investments. These are assets such as stocks, bonds, and real estate. You invest in these instruments with the expectation of capital appreciation, dividends, and interest.

People are less familiar with non-traditional investments. An example might be a private institutional fund with exposure to commercial real estate. There is a much higher level of due diligence required to access private investments. But it is a way for our clients to access a fund where normally the minimum investment is too high for them to participate. It can provide exposure to high-end real estate across the country with far less capital than would normally be needed to invest in 500 properties.

This type of investment is geared toward investors who can commit a portion of their money to a time period of one to five years, with little liquidity. The goal of alternative investments is to provide exposure to an asset class that is not correlated to the stock and bond markets. Other examples might include private equity and private debt.

Private equity is not publicly listed or traded. Private equity firms raise their own money and then invest it. After raising a certain amount, the fund is closed to new investors. It is usually liquidated after a pre-set time frame, such as ten years.

Private debt is similar—it's debt held by private companies outside of traditional companies, outside of banks, etc. There is a secondary market even for this kind of outside-the-public debt, where investors can buy the debt or even own shares in private debt funds.[30] Private debt funds raise money from investors to lend to companies with private debt—again, these are investing instruments that are not available in public markets, and fall outside the realm of traditional investments. What makes them attractive is that they often don't behave the same way as traditional assets, which can mean both more risk and more reward, but by using them as a balance to your more traditional assets, they can provide some nice side benefits to your overall plan.

Using alternative funds means we sometimes have to engage in education for our clients because so many people seem to be obsessed with traditional investments. We, however, believe strongly your money should be managed in a similar way as large endowments and pension plans. Those institutions do not have all their money in stocks or bonds, and neither should you.

Look at it this way. Suppose 25 percent of your portfolio is invested in alternative investments, 25 percent in bonds, and 50

---

[30] PitchBook Blog. PitchBook. February 5, 2020. "What is private debt?" https://pitchbook.com/blog/what-is-private-debt

percent is invested in stocks. If the stock market goes down, only half of your portfolio is exposed. This is why we believe it is better to have a diversified portfolio—one that relies on multiple asset classes—than to have 100 percent of your assets invested into the stock market.

Options

For decades, the word *"options"* has had negative connotations. The first thing that comes to everyone's mind when investing options are mentioned is options are an aggressive, speculative way to invest. That may be true, depending on your strategy. But you can say that about virtually any investment. In a properly diversified portfolio, used the right way and implemented with the correct mechanism, options can actually make a portfolio more conservative, depending on the strategy.

An option is a contract that gives the investor an "option" to buy or sell a stock or share of a fund at a predetermined price in a certain period of time. It's somewhat like planning for a stock to increase or decrease in a given time, and profiting from the situation if you are right. It can also hedge against losses if you have a particular holding that causes you concern—you can buy an option of selling it in a way that can keep you ahead of the game even if that asset itself loses money.

We use several investing strategies for our clients, but two of those option strategies, as explained below, differentiate us from other financial advisers. One type is the covered calls strategy, and the second form of option strategy we implement is selling cash-secured puts. We carefully select the companies with which we implement these options, and we typically sell covered call options on a monthly basis. We use these different options as a means of hedging, diluting risk, and improving a client's cash flow.

These two types of option strategies achieve a couple of objectives. First, they create the discipline to sell a stock if it exceeds upside expectations in a certain time period. Second, by committing to sell, we generate an immediate capital gain or cash flow that increases income in a portfolio.

Covered Call Option Strategy

The purpose of a covered call strategy is to generate income on a stock you own. It involves owning a stock and selling call options on the same stock. If you sold one call option on the stock you own, you would effectively be agreeing to sell one hundred shares of the stock at an agreed-upon price, known as the strike price. You would earn up-front income for selling the option. In this way, you are essentially investing within an investment, in a sort of stock inception. You sell shares of the share you own in order to gain immediate income rather than simply waiting until your stock pays you a dividend.

The objective is to take a basket of stocks with an average dividend of around 2 percent and increase the overall cash flow to a 6 to 8 percent range by implementing the covered call strategy on a monthly basis. By implementing the covered call strategy, we have increased income without increasing downside risk.

Let's take stock ABC, for example. Let's say we buy it at $100 a share. If we believe the stock price will go up to $107 in a month, we sell it. The old way to sell would be to put in a sell order of $107. This old way would only generate $107 dollars at the time it was bought, which is pretty straightforward. A more dynamic way to sell is by using a covered call option set at a strike price of $107 to generate an immediate premium. The buyer of the option pays the premium, and you, as the seller of the options, will collect that premium as cash flow. We have effectively capped the upside of the stock for that one-month period, meaning we will have to take action and sell the share if its value reaches this $107 cap. So, we have upside risk—if the share ultimately sells for much more than $107, we've missed that opportunity— but no additional downside risk. If the stock were to drop to $90, our downside would be the same whether we implemented the covered call strategy or not.

This increases cash flow, and, thus, your income. Another advantage is it also provides an upside-sell discipline while hedging the downside risk.

Cash-Secured Put Option Strategy

The second form of option strategy we implement is *selling cash-secured puts*. Cash-secured puts refer to an uncovered position, meaning there is no underlying security associated with this kind of put option. You are selling an option to buy or sell a stock even though you may not actually hold that asset. If the asset increases, you make money from the sale of that security, and if the asset decreases, you may be obligated to buy it at its now-reduced price.

Cash-secured put options are useful in situations where we have a client with a significant cash reserve—they have the liquidity to leverage, they don't want to be losing money to inflation and opportunity costs, but they don't necessarily want to invest all of that cash in anything longer term. The goals and objectives are to invest in certain stocks at lower prices.

For example, ABC stock is priced at $100 a share. The objective is to buy it if it drops to $95 per share. Now, the old way of investment management is to put in a buy order at $95. Maybe it gets there, maybe it doesn't. Either way, you are waiting until the price drops to receive any income based on the share. The more advanced way to buy would be to use options. With the cash-secured put option, you would sell a cash-secured put, going out for thirty days, at a strike price of $95.

As an example, let's say you sell a put at a strike price of $95 and collect $1 per share (or $1,000) on 1,000 shares. You've obligated yourself to purchase this stock if it drops to $95. In essence, you are comfortable buying the stock at a $95 price. But, while you are waiting to see if the stock dips to that point, you are rewarding yourself with additional income, as you make money from selling the put option.

One of two things will happen. If the stock does not dip to $95, I apply the same strategy next month. If it does drop to $95, I then purchase the stock. This is why it is advisable to have a favorable view of the stock you are selling a cash-secured put on, since you might end up having to buy it. Either way, though, the cash generated from selling the put is kept in your account.

Both methods, when used properly (along with the client's understanding of the risk), create a higher level of cash flow along with the discipline to sell on the upside or buy on the downside.

We use covered calls and cash-secured puts to generate additional cash flow just in case markets go sideways. We look at stock portfolios the same way real estate investors invest.

They invest in apartment buildings and seek long-term appreciating, focusing on cash flow with the monthly rental income.

When you use a covered call strategy, there are two ways to take money—capital appreciation on the underlying stock and income generated by selling options. One we can control (option-generated income), and the other we cannot. Capital appreciation is out of our control, but we expect it over the long term. In the short term, we focus on cash flow, similar to rental income. The use of covered call options and cash-secured put options is our way of doing that.

Keep in mind, options are not the only method we use for clients. In fact, there are six different categories of investment strategies we employ. Four of them involve investing in traditional stocks and bonds with no options. The other two are those that we use with options trading, which we call "dynamic" and "enhanced."

We know, this is somewhat next-level investing, and these may not be strategies you are used to hearing about. But that's part of why it's important to check these ideas out—there are strategies that are frequently used by institutional investors, like banks, endowments, foundations, and other massive entities managing huge amounts of money and trying to make the most of it. We hope that by making some of these investing strategies more accessible, we can help people like you have a better chance at competing and making the most of their money.

CHAPTER 6
Taxable, Tax-Deferred, and Tax-Free

It's big news—sometimes with a lot of controversy and anger—when word gets out some billionaire or multinational company paid less taxes than you paid last year, or maybe even *no* taxes.

Warren Buffet famously notes that, despite consistently ranking as one of the top five or top ten most wealthy Americans, he "pays fewer taxes, on a percentage basis, than his secretary and other employees, since a bulk of his wealth is in stock rather than wage income."[31]

Ordinary people don't generally get tax breaks like that. But, it's our job as your financial adviser to make sure you pay the least amount of taxes possible. The way we do that is by advising you on how and where to invest your money.

---

[31] Michelle Fox. CNBC. February 22, 2019. "Here Are 5 Ways the Super-Rich Manage to Pay Lower Taxes." https://www.cnbc.com/2019/02/21/here-are-5-ways-the-super-rich-manage-to-pay-lower-taxes.html

There are three distinct ways to set aside money—taxable accounts, tax deferred accounts, and tax-free accounts. Having money in taxable accounts is good, money in tax-deferred accounts is better, and having money in tax-free accounts is, in our opinion, usually the best. Let's start this chapter with a discussion of the positives and negatives of each.

Taxable Accounts

An easy way to describe a taxable account is as an investment account, usually at a brokerage. Your money would generally be invested in stocks, bonds, mutual funds, or exchange-traded funds. You will owe taxes on any gains realized. The nature of these taxable accounts is you will pay taxes on any taxable dividends or interest received.

Taxable accounts are going to be the most liquid, with regards to access to funds, and these are generally leveraged through individual or joint brokerage accounts, corporate accounts, or trust accounts.

It's money you can access at any time without restrictions. It will grow long-term, but, of course, taxes will have to be taken into consideration based on potential capital gains. If you invest in a stock, and it is sold at any time in the first year, you will pay short-term capital gains. If it is sold any time after that, you will pay lower long-term capital gains taxes. The positives are: You can invest and make money, and you have access to your capital immediately.

The parameters put in place to actively manage the portfolio must have a high focus on the taxes generated on the gains in the portfolio. That doesn't necessarily mean you cannot take gains. If you do take gains in these accounts, whether they are short-term or long-term gains, those gains can be offset by active portfolio management centered around tax harvesting.

Tax harvest rebalancing is the method of portfolio management centered around tax planning. If the portfolio has "paper losses," or losses from assets that lost value, like underperforming stocks, those losses can be taken, meaning you'll sell the stock and lock in those losses, to offset your capital gains for that year or to carry forward to future years. It seems counterintuitive, but selling these assets at a loss—something you likely would have to do anyway—can both free up that money to buy better-performing assets *and* allow you to use the losses to avoid paying taxes on your assets that performed well. Capital losses can even be carried forward from tax year to tax year if you have more than what can be useful for offsetting your gains.

Tax-Deferred Accounts

In accounts where your money grows tax-deferred, the taxes are not due until the money is withdrawn. Individual Retirement Accounts (IRAs), 401(k)s, 403(b)s, and annuities fall into this category.

Here's how they work: If your annual income this year is $100,000, and you contribute $6,000 to a tax-deferred account, you would pay tax on only $94,000 of income this year. When you retire, let's say your income is only $50,000 then. If you decide you need to withdraw $10,000 from the account, your taxable income would be bumped up to $60,000. Thus, you had a tax advantage while you were younger and had higher earnings, and you waited until your income was lower to take the distribution and, thus, the tax hit.

One positive of the tax-deferred account is the compound growth effect—the money can grow more efficiently because it is not taxed until it is withdrawn. Some negatives, though, are how eventually you will have to withdraw the money and pay taxes.

You are forced to take distributions from tax-deferred accounts after you reach a certain age in the U.S. These distributions are called "required minimum distributions," or RMDs. This is Uncle Sam's way of making sure you withdraw your money and pay the taxes eventually. The thinking behind this initially was, by the time you retired, you would be in a lower tax bracket because you were no longer working. Today, that is not always the case. People are retiring later and working longer.

Among the negatives of tax-deferred accounts are early withdrawal penalties and a tax hit people can still be surprised by when they make withdrawals. There are also annual limits to how much you can contribute in any given year.

Another problem is people sometimes forget taxes will have to be paid on the funds when they begin making disbursements or withdrawals. Let's look at a hypothetical example:

John has been a great saver for all his adult life. In fact, he was an enthusiastic contributor to his company's 401(k). By the time he retired six months ago, he had $600,000 saved in his 401(k). But he had little saved outside of that company-sponsored defined-contribution plan.

Well, John has always dreamed of spending his retirement with his wife, fishing. He was finally able to afford that fishing boat he had been dreaming of. He found one for $109,000 and promptly withdrew that amount, plus another $10,000 to transport his new boat to his home in California.

Big mistake! John was sixty-two, so there was no penalty for early withdrawals from the IRA. But, John's wife was still working, and he had just recently retired. As a result, they were in the 22 percent federal tax bracket. That meant Uncle Sam would get $26,000 off the top of his 401(k) withdrawal. Another 8 percent to 10 percent would then go to state taxes. That meant John would need to withdraw an excess of $150,000 to buy his $109,000 dream fishing boat.

What's the lesson? It's clear John and his wife did not have someone to help them with financial planning. As a result, all their savings were in tax-deferred accounts. Apparently, John forgot those accounts are tax-deferred, *not tax-free.* He put all his eggs in the tax-deferred bucket. That was a mistake. And that is why we help our clients understand the necessity of using all three tax buckets.

Tax-Free Accounts

The last bucket is tax-free accounts. We think it is the best way to save money, since this money has already been taxed. When you use a tax-free account, you are using after-tax dollars to invest in buckets where earnings are all growing tax-free. Your contributions to a tax-free account are taxed at your normal tax rate *before* the money goes into the account.

One example is a Roth IRA. The problem is there are strict limitations on what you can set aside in a Roth account. There are limits on how much you can earn in order to be eligible to participate in contributing to a Roth. But there are also new rules allowing investors to convert tax-deferred IRAs to tax-free IRAs.

There is no financial advice that would apply to everyone. But it is a good idea for young investors to put money into Roth accounts if they can. Having your money grow tax-free for a long period of time gives you the advantage of potentially higher capital appreciation (based on historical returns of stocks).

Older investors who want to convert their tax-deferred accounts to tax-free accounts can pay the taxes today, and then let the money grow tax-free. But you need to do a break-even analysis based on your age and projected taxes to see if it makes sense for you to convert in this fashion.

You might be lucky enough to have an employer who offers a 401(k) Roth in their corporate plan. In this type of account, you get the same tax advantages without the income restrictions. Your money can grow completely tax-free. The Roth 401(k) has the same contribution limit as a traditional 401(k), which is generally three times higher than a regular IRA.

You may also have access to another type of tax-exempt account through your employer—a health savings account (HSA). It is typically used to pay for qualified medical expenses, such as vision services, dental care, and hearing aids, as well as the following:

- It can also be used to pay for some Medicare expenses, such as Part B and Part D (prescription-drug coverage).

- For retirees over age sixty-five with employer-sponsored health plans, it can be used to pay the employee share of premium costs.

- It can be used to cover part of the cost for a long-term care insurance policy.

Thus, not only are HSA accounts useful as tax-free accounts, they can also play a valuable part in a portfolio that uses taxable, tax-deferred, and tax-free accounts.

As we've outlined here, the bucket your money is positioned in can make a significant difference in your overall financial picture. Relying on money that has never been taxed means having to plan to withdraw more than what you need in order to pay the taxes on that money. Knowing where your money is and how it will be taxed is key in developing strategies to plan in advance for your income and investment needs. It's crucial to work with a financial adviser who can help you navigate this area in a way that helps you keep more of your own hard-earned money in your pockets.

CHAPTER 7
Accumulation of Wealth vs. Distribution of Wealth

When it comes to retirement, there are two very distinct stages of your financial life. The first is your savings phase, which we call "the accumulation of wealth." The second stage is what we refer to as "the distribution of wealth," referring, basically, to when you retire and start to take distributions from your retirement savings—be it pensions, 401(k)s, TSAs (for government employees), IRAs, or just regular savings.

These two stages require completely different strategies and philosophies. And, even if a client makes it through the first phase without a financial adviser, it would be highly advisable to seek financial help when it comes to replacing your weekly, or bi-weekly, paycheck with distributions (or withdrawals) from your savings.

Both phases seem to scare the heck out of Americans. In fact, 49 percent of Americans (of all ages) say their biggest fear is outliving their savings.[32] In that same survey, 44 percent worried about declining health in connection with longevity concerns.[33]

Those fears are probably justified for many, considering:

- 21 percent of Americans do not save any of their income, and even those who do aren't saving nearly enough.[34]

- More than 40 percent of Americans have saved less than $10,000 for retirement.[35]

Longevity also comes into play. Americans are living into their eighties and nineties—longer than their parents and grandparents. So, it's entirely possible you will spend as much time in retirement as you did in your working life.

Accumulation

The sooner you start saving, the better. But that doesn't mean you are doomed if you didn't start in your twenties and thirties. Sometimes life gets in the way. Between student loans, marriage, having children, and buying a house, some people don't start seriously saving until their late forties or fifties.

---

[32] Harriet Edleson. *AARP*. May 21, 2019. "Almost Half of Americans Fear Running Out of Money in Retirement." https://www.aarp.org/retirement/planning-for-retirement/info-2019/retirees-fear-losing-money.html
[33] Ibid.
[34] Amanda Dixon. Bankrate. March 14, 2019. "Survey: 21% of working Americans aren't saving anything at all." https://www.bankrate.com/banking/savings/financial-security-march-2019/
[35] Emmie Martin. CNBC. March 4, 2018. "65% of Americans save little or nothing—and half could end up struggling in retirement." https://www.cnbc.com/2018/03/15/bankrate-65-percent-of-americans-save-little-or-nothing.html

Ultimately, every person's situation is unique and different. It has to do with their personal lifestyle, expenses, and the type of lifestyle they expect to have in retirement. Our definition of saving is not putting money into a savings account but, rather, investing to outpace inflation and grow your wealth.

Just 39 percent of adults, who are saving for retirement, started in their twenties. Slightly more than a quarter of Americans began saving in their thirties. Fifteen percent began saving in their forties and 6 percent in their fifties.[36]

Again, let us emphasize this: It is never too late to start saving to invest. The key is to set aside enough to build your wealth so, by the time you are retired, you have enough saved to replace the income you will no longer have from your former employer.

Compound Interest

"Compound interest is the eighth wonder of the world. He who understands it, earns it; he who doesn't, pays it." – Albert Einstein

For purposes of saving and investing, compound interest is the addition of interest to the principal sum of deposit—basically interest paid on interest. The interest in the following year is earned on the principal plus the previously earned interest (or the principal including previously earned interest).

Say you invest $10,000 at 10 percent interest. At the end of the year, your $10,000, with $1,000 in interest, becomes $11,000. If you

---

[36] Alicia Adamczyk. CNBC. September 4, 2019. "This is when people start saving for retirement—and when they actually should."
https://www.cnbc.com/2019/09/04/the-age-when-americans-start-saving-for-retirement.html

reinvest that $1,000, still at 10 percent interest, your $11,000 grows to $12,100 in the second year. You are, in effect, gaining interest on interest.

Now, let's assume you have $100,000 invested at the same 10 percent interest rate. Even if you don't add any more money to your principal, in twenty years, with compound interest, you would have $672,749.

To make it easier for you to determine how compound interest may play into your individual situation, compound interest calculators are easily found at many financial sites on the web.

The Rule of 72

The Rule of 72 is an easy way to determine how long it will take your investment to double with a fixed interest rate. Divide seventy-two by the annual interest or rate of return in your account. Using a 10 percent rate, your investment would double in 7.2 years. The numbers aren't exact, but it will give you a good idea of where you will stand.

The reason we discuss things such as compound interest and the Rule of 72 is not to make things complicated but to make this point: The earlier you start saving, the more money you are likely to have when you decide to retire.

Risk

During accumulation, one must be aware of managing risk, but the bigger risk is being too conservative in your method of investing.

There is a fine line between crossing a level of risk and becoming overly speculative. But there is a huge risk in not taking on a reasonable level of chance in your investments.

We prefer to use the term "asset accumulation" rather than saving. Savings implies putting your money in a bank account or bank CD. But, if you are not significantly outpacing inflation in your accumulation phase, those dollars you set aside are worth less each year.

Without getting specific about what the correct portfolio should look like, it is important you take a "reasonable" level of risk by looking at investments that outpace inflation—not just ones that keep pace with inflation.

Let's review a few examples, starting with a timeline. John starts investing at age twenty-five and does not plan to retire until age sixty-five. Clearly, he should be heavily invested in stocks at his age—he has plenty of time to recover from stock market fluctuations.

Nancy, meanwhile, waited until her fifties to start investing. Children, college, and a divorce got in her way. If she is ten years or less away from retiring, she can't possibly have the same risk in her investments as a twenty-five-year-old. We'll have to make up for that by having her increase her savings rate.

This is also where it's clear the old way of thinking about investments is outdated. The prevailing thought used to be, the older you are, the fewer stocks should be in your portfolio. That old rule of thumb said you should subtract your age from one hundred to get the percentage of your portfolio that should be in stocks. For example, if you're sixty, you should keep 40 percent of your portfolio in stocks.

Today, things are different. We would say Suzy, who started investing at forty-five, and Tom, who waited until age fifty-two to start investing for retirement, should both have some exposure to stocks for long-term growth. Ultimately, the bigger risk in being too conservative is your money is not working for you, and, if you do live a long life, you may ultimately run out of money.

In our experience, retirees tend to make the same mistake younger savers make—being too conservative.

That old rule dictating how you should hold a percentage of stocks equal to one hundred minus your age may have worked for your father, but, based on what we've seen in our practice, it is likely bad advice for you today.

We are living much longer now due to healthier lifestyles and advances in medicine. The old strategy could be an easy way for you to run out of money before you die—Americans' biggest fear. In fact, a recent *Wall Street Journal* article lists investing too conservatively as the number one mistake in "The Biggest Financial Mistakes Retirees Make."[37]

"Though taking a more conservative approach in retirement can be prudent, playing it *too* safe can severely limit retirees' earning potential, increasing the chances they'll run out of money," the story says.[38]

Today, your retirement portfolio needs to be managed with the objective of both growth and income. Things are different today

---

[37] Cheryl Winokur Munk. *The Wall Street Journal*. April 21, 2019. "The Biggest Financial Mistakes Retirees Make." https://www.wsj.com/articles/the-biggest-financial-mistakes-retirees-make-11555898940
[38] Ibid.

with retirees living well into their eighties and nineties. What worked fifty years ago just doesn't work today.

If at sixty-five there is no growth on your principal and your income needs remains the same, the effects of inflation over time will erode the power of each dollar in your account. This in turn means that, by the time you are seventy-five, you may need $1.18 to cover each dollar of income you needed ten years ago. Without growth in your account, you'll need to dip you're your principal amount sooner rather than later, and the sooner that you break into that principal, the less likely that your portfolio will last for the duration of what you likely hope to be a long and independent retirement. That is why your portfolio needs to be managed with the objective of both growth and income.

The right financial adviser can guide you through both phases of your life. Think of it like you think of your doctor. Your primary physician knows just about everything about you. He or she has known you throughout the years and through the different stages of your life. Your doctor knows your allergies and which vaccinations you've had, any surgeries you may have undergone, and what diseases you may be prone to.

As holistic advisers, we understand the value of a *specialist* being brought in occasionally. But a true holistic adviser will work with clients through each and every stage of their lives. When you graduate college, your expenses are low. As you get older, you buy an auto, get married, have children, and buy a home. As such, your financial needs are different in every phase. We believe strongly a holistic adviser should be able to work with a client through each of those different stages.

Distribution

People often save for years and are nearing retirement before they first think about distributions. The fact is, figuring out how to withdraw from your retirement accounts in a way consistent with keeping your tax liability low is important even when you are still saving.

Having a financial plan with a strategy for saving as well as a strategy for investing can help alleviate fears of running out of money in retirement. Withdrawing from retirement savings accounts with an eye toward reducing taxes is important. Taxes can reduce income as well as diminish potential future earnings and growth, which affect how long savings may last.

As we've already stated in an earlier chapter, a typical retiree may have three types of accounts: taxable, tax-deferred, and tax-free. Each has an important, but different, role to play in helping manage tax exposure in retirement.

The goal is to manage your withdrawals with the help of your financial adviser in order to help reduce taxes and maximize the ability of remaining investments to grow tax-efficiently.

The simplest, most basic withdrawal strategy is to use money from savings and retirement accounts in the order below, with one important caveat. For certain retirement accounts, if you are seventy-two or older, required minimum distributions (RMDs) come first. For inherited qualified accounts like a traditional IRA, the rules are complex, so check with your tax professional. Here are a few basic rules for each type of account:

1. Taxable accounts: Typically, they are the least tax-efficient of the three, which is why it usually makes sense to withdraw

the money in these accounts first. This allows qualified retirement accounts to continue growing and generating tax-deferred or tax-free earnings.

2. Tax-deferred accounts: These accounts require you to pay ordinary income taxes when you withdraw from them, but they will have extra time to grow if you take withdrawals from a taxable account first. The expectation is you will be in a lower income tax bracket as you age, so the tax on your withdrawals could be less.

3. Tax-free accounts: The longer these accounts are untouched, the longer the potential for them to generate tax-free earnings. Withdrawals, in most cases, won't be subject to ordinary income tax.

Remember, the strategies for saving and investing that got you to retirement are not going to be the same strategies that will get you through retirement—accumulating those savings is very different than managing the responsible and lifelong distribution of them.

CHAPTER 8
Tax Planning

When it comes to taxes, there is tax planning, and then there is tax preparation. It's important you understand the difference.

Tax preparation is done by accountants who gather information on what's happened in the past. They input that data into their software systems to determine if additional taxes are owed or if a refund from the government is due.

Tax planning is the work done in advance—before tax preparation. The proper role of a holistic fiduciary adviser is to factor in the taxes for a client or a family throughout the year as the adviser actively manages their portfolio.

To do this properly, your financial adviser needs to have the right tools and technology to hopefully minimize the work done ahead of tax preparation. To have an effective tax planning strategy, your financial adviser and your accountant must communicate clearly with each other.

Proper Tax Planning Is Not Seasonal

A client can have multiple strategies and accounts in their portfolio, and your adviser should be prepared for that. For example, you may have ABC stock in one account your financial adviser is looking to sell. Your adviser needs to make sure new shares of ABC are not purchased in another account for at least thirty days. Without details like this, the effectiveness of tax planning is diminished.

Many financial advisers do not take this into consideration until the last two weeks of the calendar year when they book investment losses. This is not the way to do tax planning. Proper tax planning is not seasonal. It must happen throughout the entire year.

Ultimately, the net return to the client is not just calculated after fees, but after tax liability. As much as we may dislike taxes, we cannot avoid them. If tax planning is indeed a part of your strategy through the calendar year, not just the end of the year, you should be able to minimize your exposure to taxes or, at the very least, avoid some unnecessary taxes. That is crucial.

A fiduciary adviser should also be asking you about investments outside of their office's management so they are aware of gains and losses in those portfolios. Often, clients have multiple accounts, sometimes at multiple different institutions. For example, some clients may have one account managed by their investment adviser and may still be contributing to a 401(k) or 403(b) through their company or university. A good adviser should be asking about carry-forward losses from tax returns, and they should be knowledgeable enough to review tax returns and understand actions taken by an investor in the past.

Stay Up-to-Date on Tax Laws

Tax law changes may happen annually, but they certainly occur when there is a new administration in the White House. Proposals are constantly being made in Congress, especially with various changes in leadership. It is the responsibility of a fiduciary adviser to understand these changes so they can reconstruct your portfolio and make changes to the types of rebalancing used and the types of securities invested in.

For example, suppose the capital gains tax is reduced to 10 percent, regardless of income or long-term capital gains. That's a huge change—what we might call "a big deal." It's also a case where you must have a sophisticated system in place for your financial adviser to help you take advantage of this new opportunity.

Suppose taxes on dividend income go up. Fiduciary advisers should look at your portfolio, taking into consideration the new higher taxes on those types of investments.

For example, The Tax Cuts and Jobs Act of 2017 issued historic tax legislation. That legislation, passed in December 2017, made major changes to the individual income tax, nearly doubled standard deduction, created new limits on itemized deductions, reduced income tax rates, and introduced reforms to several other provisions.

After December 31, 2025, most of the changes to the individual income tax code revert to pre-legislation status. If the U.S. Congress allows these changes to revert back to their pre-2017 state, most households will experience tax increases beginning in 2026.

Historic legislation like this requires your financial adviser to keep track of changes in codes and regulations to judge the impact on clients even before it is passed into law. This necessity dramatically changes the way we do our tax planning. We need to be prepared, and we certainly are.

Other things may happen mid-year, usually centered around market conditions. If the stock market is in a negative position in the first half of the year and there are paper losses—losses you wouldn't lock in unless you sell those assets while they are down—we would want to utilize those losses for the second half of the year. No one wants losses, but when they happen, the right thing to do is to use them to offset gains and avoid higher taxes.

Ultimately, the most effective use of investing changes and tax harvesting is not a matter of an occasional review. Even if your adviser is looking at your portfolio three times a year, that is not enough. Again, with proper use of technology, your adviser can identify capital gains and have triggers in place to gauge if an investment is exceeding a certain threshold. We might, for example, put a trigger in place to alert us when a client's capital gains exceed $100,000. An adviser with a large client base would find it impossible to do this if they did not have that technology in place. It all goes back to working with the right financial adviser who uses sophisticated software and can customize each client's triggers to see when the gains are exceeding their individual threshold.

We work with our clients' accountants on an as-needed basis. That's important. They are more involved in preparation and less involved in planning. We are not in any way discounting or disparaging accountants. We are only trying to point out how they are often only looking at information from the past instead of planning ahead to help save on future taxation.

Mutual Funds and Capital Gains

Let's end this discussion of taxes with a discussion of some pitfalls. Let's start with mutual funds. They are a pitfall, and here's why. You can be invested in a mutual fund, hold it, and never sell a share. But, you will still have to pay capital gains taxes on distributions by the fund manager. You can buy a mutual fund today and the fund manager decides on distributions tomorrow. Still, you are responsible for the capital gains.

Now, taxes are important. But your first decision in investment planning should not, and cannot, be based around taxes. Taxes must be taken into consideration, but they cannot be the primary reason to buy or sell a stock. It is better to pay taxes on a stock that made you money than to watch the stock decline and lose money.

Sometimes It Is Okay to Sell a Stock and Pay Taxes on the Gains

Sometimes, there are people who don't necessarily have an emotional attachment to a stock but hold onto it just because they don't want to pay taxes on the gains. Yes, it's true we want to avoid paying unnecessary taxes. But, it's also okay to sell your stocks. Tax planning should certainly be a part of your investment decisions, but it should *not* be the primary reason for selling or holding a stock.

Still, there are some steps you should keep in mind to minimize or avoid capital gains taxes. The biggest step you can take is to invest for the long term. Besides avoiding the costly short-term capital gains taxes, you are also likely sticking to your financial plan better by having a long-term view.

The bottom line on taxes is that the laws are always changing, and working with a coordinated team that incorporates tax planning—and not just tax preparation—into a long-term investment plan is a necessary piece of keeping more of your hard-earned money in your pocket.

CHAPTER 9

Estate Planning

The old saying famously used by Benjamin Franklin goes something like, "Nothing can be said to be certain, except death and taxes." If that truly is the case, then Americans do not like to plan for either certainty.

According to one survey, 60 percent of Americans do not have a will and have not done any estate planning.[39] Some of the top reasons or excuses I often hear in my office for people not having a will are, "I haven't gotten around to it," and "I don't have enough money to warrant a will."

One of the reasons people avoid estate planning is because there is no immediate benefit to feel and touch. Think about buying a home/rental property or investing in stocks. In both there is a cause and visible effect. Even in retirement planning, you can see the benefits after a year or, even, after a day.

---

[39] Barbranda Lumpkins Walls. *AARP*. February 24, 2017. "Haven't Done A Will Yet?" https://www.aarp.org/money/investing/info-2017/half-of-adults-do-not-have-wills.html

Who are the people we see who tend to hesitate when it comes to estate planning? They are mostly single individuals or married couples without children. The public has a general perception of estate planning being for the rich and the old. But estate planning will benefit everyone. In simple terms, it's the proper distribution of your belongings, regardless of their value. It could be just $1,000. It could be your grandmother's china. It could be your Rolex. It doesn't have to be stocks and businesses.

Also, human psychology plays a role in the apathy toward estate planning. If I told you, in order to retire in ten years, you need to invest in these four stocks, then you would be ecstatic. But, if I tell you we want to make sure the government does not take a large chunk of your wealth upon your death, you may have a more muted reaction.

Let us start with a question. What is estate planning? Estate planning means taking steps during your life to assure the proper management and distribution of your assets, or the re-arranging of assets so taxes are minimized upon your death.

Estate planning is more about rewarding, or relieving, the next generation than it is about you. It is about the legacy you want to leave behind. The benefits of this type of planning are less for you as a client and more for your beneficiaries.

Estate planning must be an integral part of any retirement plan we create for a client. The biggest issue for those who choose to avoid estate planning is taxes. Upon their death, their estates could face taxes that could have been easily prevented. If you don't take the proper actions, taxes will be paid by your estate when they could have been potentially eliminated.

Proper estate planning allows for the management of your distribution of assets during your lifetime using techniques such as donor-advised funds or direct giving of investments or cash to family members. In estate planning there are rules that need to be followed. Because of these rules, you are prevented from waiting until you reach age ninety-nine to begin gifting. There are limitations on what you can gift per year.

Dying without a will is called dying "intestate." Intestate status means your state's particular laws of inheritance will determine how your property is distributed upon your death—the court will decide where bank accounts, securities, real estate, and any other assets go when you die.

Living Trust

In this chapter, we're talking about a basic type of estate planning that ensures your assets get distributed to the proper people. Let's take the formation of a family living trust, for example. It can be created by any family member—two sisters or a husband and wife. The purpose is to make sure, upon the death of the trustee or trustees, a successor trustee will take over the distribution of assets so the estate does not have to go through costly probate that could take up to twelve months.

Let's look at two hypothetical examples for illustration.

Example one is not tax-related but probate-related. A husband and wife have not set up a living trust. The accounts and assets they own are under the names of the individuals only.

The IRA accounts act as a trust by themselves—they pass directly to the beneficiary. But let's look at the non-retirement accounts. Without a trust, upon the death of the second spouse, the assets will enter probate. That costs from 2 to 5 percent of the value of the estate, depending on what state you're in and what kind of legal representation you may need. That could mean paying $50,000 on a $1 million estate that could have been avoided with a trust. In addition, the beneficiary is left waiting for the distribution.[40]

On top of this, people who are not entitled to the assets could step in and say they are entitled to part of the estate. Now the husband and wife are putting themselves in the position of having a judge decide if those claims are valid. If there was a trust in place, there would be no question. It would be a direct transfer of assets to a named beneficiary of the trust. No one could come in and say, "The deceased told me this." And, if the burden was not enough on the family already, the family must pay additional legal costs if non-family members come in and say they are entitled to part of the estate.

Example two concerns proper gifting for a client whose spouse has died and who has no children. His estate is valued at $40 million. When he passes away, some will go to charity, some will go to friends, and a good amount will go to taxes.

His mistake was not doing the proper planning—not gifting early and not utilizing life insurance when he was still insurable and in good health. Thus, he is swarmed with unnecessary taxes. Insurance could have been used as a valuable investment tool for him, one that could have paid his beneficiaries tax-free money.

Suppose Jim and Donna are married and have an estate that would owe $10 million in taxes if they were to die today. They

---

[40] Fidelity. 2020. "Settling the Estate: Probate."
https://myguidance.fidelity.com/ftgw/pna/public/lifeevents/content/losing-a-loved-one/overview/setting-estate-after-death

decide to purchase a second-to-die insurance policy and put it outside of the estate in an irrevocable trust. Then, upon the death of the second spouse, the proceeds will be paid outside of the estate to the irrevocable trust. This way, the beneficiaries could use that money to pay estate taxes due and avoid any other unnecessary taxes or fees.

Take an Active Approach to Planning

The mistakes we often see are families not taking an active approach to planning and not starting early. Also, there are those who have an estate value that may fall below the threshold of estate tax laws, but they may not have factored in the growth of their assets. That estate may fall into the taxable category at some point in the future, which could incur unnecessary taxes.

Another mistake is not actively updating their living trust. People may have set up their trust provisions when their children were younger. Ten years later, the children are in their twenties, and perhaps there are now grandchildren they want to include in their planning.

It's incumbent on each person to review their living trusts every five years or, at least, when there are life-changing events.

It's more than just about passing wealth to the next generation. It's also outlining who will take care of young children if both partners pass away. This is how parents can ensure their child (or children) are raised by the person they select. And, settling these issues before a time of emotional crisis will avoid possible family fights and hard feelings that may otherwise drag on for years.

Living Will

A living will, also called a "directive to physicians" or an "advance directive," is a document that lets people state their wishes for end-of-life medical care in case they become unable to communicate their decisions.

The document also allows a person to appoint a health care representative to act on their behalf to carry out these wishes. Although state laws can vary, living wills generally do not expire while their subjects are alive, absent special circumstances or that person's express intent.

Types of advance directives:

- **The living will.** A living will provides instructions regarding end-of-life care. It lets you make your own choices about life support and helps prevent confusion about the type of care you do, or do not, want in the event you become incapable of communicating your wishes. Without a living will, the laws in your state will determine who will make your health care decisions.

- **Medical power of attorney/Durable power of attorney for health care.** This is a legal document giving a person you select the power to act in your place if you become mentally incapacitated. You should have durable powers of attorney for both medical care and finances.

- **Physician orders for life-sustaining treatment (POLST).** This is an end-of-life planning tool utilized when your physician expects you to live a year or less. It would contain your instructions for medical treatments for specific health-related emergencies or conditions based on decisions made by you and your doctor. They exist at some level in all fifty states and Washington D.C.

- **Do not resuscitate (DNR) order.** This is a legal document telling your family what kind of care you want if you are in a coma, are seriously injured, fall ill, or have dementia.

- **Organ and tissue donation.** This is pretty self-explanatory. When you legally allow an organ or tissue to be transplanted to another with the consent of your next of kin, you are employing an advance directive.

Passing More Than Just Dollars

There are parts of estate planning that many either forget or overlook. The generation passing the wealth should not be passing on just dollars or assets.

Many times, a person has spent decades building the wealth they leave their heirs or charities. We tell people to take their time and explain to their heirs what it took to get to that level. It was probably a long and arduous journey. A person should tell their heirs why they made the decisions they made. It is especially easy today to record videos on a phone or tablet, so there's no reason for a person not to take a few minutes to explain themselves for the next generation.

However a person goes about doing it, it's important to personally explain, in their own words, how they created their wealth wish heirs will take care of it to maintain it for future generations.

We remind people to be sure, whatever your plans are, to work in conjunction with your estate planning attorney and financial adviser to be sure your wishes are known and will be carried out.

CHAPTER 10
Insurance Planning

The concept of wealth management, from a holistic point of view, involves looking at all types of assets to formulate a plan to help a client navigate through different elements of life and changing circumstances. Such a review includes assets, liabilities, and insurance.

The outcome is portfolio management, investment planning, and debt management, but an important part of looking at the needs of our clients includes insurance. When it comes to wealth management, we are looking at insurance that can be used to protect our clients from the loss of income, to protect them from the risk of estate taxes, or to protect them from high expenses associated with long-term care.

For our clients, risk management under the umbrella of insurance planning would include life insurance, disability insurance, and long-term care insurance.

Part of insurance planning is determining the cost-benefit analysis. We do not want to overinsure or underinsure.

Does everyone need life insurance? No. Part of the process of financial planning is to determine life insurance on an as-needed basis. A proper needs analysis looks at what would be the loss of income to the family if there was a premature death of one or both spouses, especially when children are involved.

For example, say you have a married couple, John and Suzy. John makes $100,000 a year, and Suzy makes $300,000. Let's say they have two children, ages eight and ten, and the family's yearly expenses after taxes are $200,000.

The risk to the family lies in if the higher-paid parent passes away. There would be a loss of income of $300,000. That must be replaced in order for the family to continue paying their yearly expenses. If the family has substantial assets set aside that can cover expenses over a period—say, until the children reach adulthood—insurance may not be needed.

But it's not as simple as that. Even if there are other sources of income and access to capital, the need for life insurance may still exist. If Suzy and John are still building wealth and don't have access to those accounts, the need for life insurance would be greater.

The next question is how much insurance, what type, and at what cost? How much will be based on a formula. We would need to run metrics to determine the loss of income, assets, age of the individuals, and how many dependents they have.

If we determine Suzy needs $1 million in insurance, what is the amount we can afford to invest in this policy that will not affect her family's current lifestyle? If the money is going to insurance, that means it is not going someplace else. The money may have been going into savings or towards private school tuition. There must be a cost analysis because, once you determine what type of insurance to use, the cost comes into play.

Life Insurance

There are two basic types of insurance—permanent and term life insurance. Having only two options sounds simple, but the complexity comes into play because of the many different forms each option comes in.

Term life insurance provides you with a predetermined death benefit that covers you for a fixed number of years, usually ranging from five years to thirty years. Premiums can be calculated monthly or annually, and they are based on your health and your life expectancy at the time you are initially insured.

Permanent life insurance is basically insurance guaranteed for the rest of your life. It combines a death benefit with a savings or investment account. This can make the policy somewhat complicated for some people. But, the death benefit part of the insurance policy will cover you for the rest of your life—even if you live to be one hundred. Depending on the policy, the premiums may or may not be fixed. And, like term life insurance, the premiums are based on your health and medical history at the time you are insured.

Permanent insurance is much more costly. If you think about it, the insurance company is guaranteeing you payment for the rest of your life, which is typically an expensive action on their part.

There are certain situations when a term policy may be the most cost-effective option for a younger family. But, if they will be using insurance as a means of providing additional income to loved ones or to pay taxes, permanent insurance may be the best option.

Your permanent policy may be invested in a fixed account (a universal policy) or invested in the stock market (variable). We believe insurance should be invested conservatively and should not be invested directly into the stock market.

We use the same six-step process mentioned in previous chapters to determine the need for life insurance and what type best suits our clients' current situation.

Health Insurance & Medicare

It's easy for pre-retirees to forget to plan for health insurance. But the cost can be startling for someone who is unexpectedly hit with it. Consider how nearly 156.3 million Americans are covered by employer-based health insurance coverage.[41] In 2018, the average monthly cost of health insurance for an individual (including employer and employee contributions) was $574 per month, and family coverage averaged $1,634, according to Dave Ramsey.[42]

---

[41] KFF. February 1, 2019. "Coverage at Work: The Share of Nonelderly Americans with Employer-Based Insurance Rose Modestly in Recent Years, but Has Declined Markedly Over the Long Term." https://www.kff.org/health-reform/press-release/coverage-at-work-the-share-of-nonelderly-americans-with-employer-based-insurance-rose-modestly-in-recent-years-but-has-declined-markedly-over-the-long-term/
[42] Dave Ramsey. "How Much Does Health Insurance Cost?" https://www.daveramsey.com/blog/how-much-does-health-insurance-cost

In the most recent data available, the average employer contribution for family coverage was $14,069. The average employee share was $5,547. That's a total of $19,616:[43]

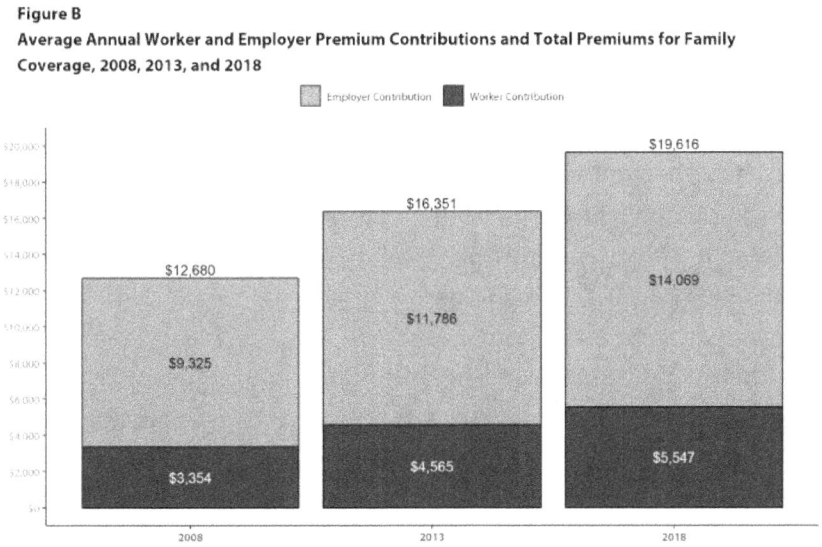

Figure B
Average Annual Worker and Employer Premium Contributions and Total Premiums for Family Coverage, 2008, 2013, and 2018

NOTE: Since 2008, the average family premium has increased 55% and the average worker contribution toward the premium has increased 65%.
SOURCE: KFF Employer Health Benefits Survey, 2018; Kaiser/HRET Survey of Employer-Sponsored Health Benefits, 2008 and 2013.

One of the biggest mistakes an early retiree can make is to forget about planning for health insurance. If they retire at age sixty-two and are not covered by a spouse, they will have to enter the open market to buy insurance until they are eligible for Medicare at sixty-five.

---

[43] KFF. October 3, 2018. "2018 Employer Health Benefits Survey." https://www.kff.org/report-section/2018-employer-health-benefits-survey-summary-of-findings/#figurea

That's where things get expensive. The average national monthly health insurance cost for one person in 2020 is $462.[44] Of course, premiums can vary by state. The cost could vary depending on your age, tobacco use, location, and your plan level.

That monthly cost could be as high as $812 in Wyoming and $622 in New York, in 2020, to $363 in California and $275 in Minnesota according to healthmarkets.com.[45]

Many people plan to retire and take Social Security early. And, even though they can retire at age sixty-two and still receive Social Security (though it will be 30 percent lower than if they retire at full retirement age), the Medicare program is not flexible. You qualify at sixty-five . . . period.

That means you are forced to find insurance for what could be a budget-busting $1,000 a month. Remember, the costs quoted earlier are an average, and, once you reach fifty years old, health care premiums are considerably higher.

From *The Street:*

"At age fifty-three, the average premium is more than double the base rate, and, by age fifty-five, the average monthly premium is $446. At age sixty, the average premium is $543. If a person is sixty-four years old, the average health insurance premium is $600."[46]

---

[44] Health Markets. "How Much Does Health Insurance Cost Per Month?" https://www.healthmarkets.com/content/health-insurance-cost-per-month
[45] Ibid.
[46] Steve Fiorillo. *The Street.* April 3, 2020. "Average Health Insurance Cost by Age and State." https://www.thestreet.com/personal-finance/average-health-insurance-cost-14878894

Again, all these averages will vary by state. The bottom line is, because health insurance companies expect to have to pay more for care for older people, they charge them more, too.

Once you reach age sixty-five, you are eligible for Medicare. For most Part B premiums, the monthly rate is less than $150.[47]

Disability Insurance

Everything we have mentioned about life insurance also applies to disability insurance. The difference is disability insurance protects your family from loss of income, not from death, but it provides protection when an injury or some misfortune prevents you from working.

Disability insurance is a type of insurance providing income if you are unable to perform your job due to a disability. There are many types of disability insurance, and each company will have specific rules as to what constitutes a disability and how a person qualifies to receive the benefit.

Short-term disability insurance offers you a portion of your salary if you are not able to work for a short period—typically three to six months.

Long-term disability insurance offers you a portion of your salary if you are unable to work for a longer period—typically longer than six months.

Both short-term and long-term disability policies have a certain period a person must be disabled for before that individual is

---

[47] Medicare.gov. "Part B costs." https://www.medicare.gov/your-medicare-costs/part-b-costs

able to start receiving disability benefits. If you become disabled, you must wait until that "elimination period" is over before you can begin receiving your benefits.

Long-Term Care Insurance

The cost of a private room in a nursing home varies widely depending on the state you live in, but Genworth's cost of care national estimate averages the cost out to $8,517 a month.[48] Costs like that can quickly drain your savings.

Of course, there's no way of knowing if you will need long-term care or how long you might need it. Some statistics on long-term care according to Morningstar are as follows:[49]

- The number of Americans who are expected to need long-term care by 2050: 15 million.

- The percentage of people turning sixty-five who will need long-term care at some point in their lifetimes: 52.3 percent.

- The percentage of men turning sixty-five who will need long-term care in their lifetimes: 46.7 percent.

- The percentage of women turning sixty-five who will need long-term care during their lifetimes: 57.5 percent.

---

[48] Genworth Financial. November 21, 2019. "Genworth 2019 Cost of Care Survey." https://www.genworth.com/aging-and-you/finances/cost-of-care.html

[49] Christine Benz. Morningstar. August 31, 2017. "75 Must-Know Statistics About Long-Term Care." https://www.morningstar.com/articles/823957/75-must-know-statistics-about-long-term-care

You should consider protecting yourself against this potentially devastating expense with long-term care insurance.

Most people don't carry long-term care insurance because it's expensive. There has also been considerable controversy over premium increases on older long-term care insurance policies. There have been many cases of people who have paid for the policies for years only to have to give them up in retirement—when they needed them the most—because they could no longer afford to pay the costly premiums.

Also, most people need to buy insurance on their own because few employers offer them—so there's no subsidy. One group estimates only 16 percent of people over age sixty-five who are looking for long-term insurance solutions actually go with a traditional long-term care insurance policy. [50]

If you were to need assistance and believe your spouse would not be capable of providing care, or you would not want to put that burden on your spouse or children, we analyze the cost of long-term care insurance for you and what impact it could have on your financial plan.

We help you determine if it makes sense to shift some of your money into a bucket that could be used for long-term care in the future.

---

[50] American Association for Long-Term Care Insurance. March 25, 2019. "Long-Term Care Insurance Buyers; 350,000 in 2018."

CHAPTER 11
Emotions of Investing

Investment decisions can be highly emotional. That can lead to some truly terrible financial decisions.

Study after study has shown individual mutual fund investors rarely, if ever, get out of the market at the top—and they rarely get back into the market at the bottom. Instead, time and again, they end up selling low then buying high after missing an explosive start to a stock market rally.

- Investment decisions based on emotions (especially greed or fear) are the real reason many investors buy at the top of the market and sell at the bottom of the market.

- Investors often underestimate the risks associated with investing, a reason many make bad decisions that are based on excessive emotions.

- When markets are volatile and interest rates are rising, individual investors generally move their money from stocks to low-risk securities.

Let's take a minute and look at the lessons history has taught us. You don't have to be very old to remember the devastation caused by the stock market crash of 2008-2009. The Dow Jones Industrial Average fell 777.68 points on September 29, 2008, which (back then) was the biggest point drop in history.[51] By March 5, 2009, it was down more than 50 percent to 6,594.44.[52]

According to *The Atlantic*, "The nation's 401(k)s and IRAs lost about $2.4 trillion in the final two quarters of 2008, and the average loss that year for workers who had been on the job for twenty years was, according to one estimate, about 25 percent."[53]

You may be asking: Why are we bringing up a crash that happened so long ago? The answer is because the aftermath of that market bloodbath exemplifies what we are talking about when we discuss emotional investing.

Ten years after that market crash, the DJIA had delivered a ten-year annualized total return of 17.8 percent.[54] In the same time an all-cash portfolio returned more like 2 percent. The people who were spooked out of the market missed out on huge gains.

In fact, a survey done by T. Rowe Price study said stock markets have recovered from every downturn—despite depressions, world wars, and recessions—including the 2008 to 2009

---

[51] Kimberly Amadeo. *The Balance*. April 20, 2020. "The Stock Market Crash of 2008." https://www.thebalance.com/stock-market-crash-of-2008-3305535
[52] Ibid.
[53] Teresa Ghilarducci. *The Atlantic*. October 16, 2015. "The Recession Hurt Americans' Retirement Accounts More Than Anybody Knew." https://www.theatlantic.com/business/archive/2015/10/the-recession-hurt-americans-retirement-accounts-more-than-everyone-thought/410791/
[54] Michael Santoli. CNBC. March 4, 2019. "10 years ago this week, the market hit the climactic bottom of the Great Recession." https://www.cnbc.com/2019/03/04/the-10th-anniversary-of-the-climactic-march-2009-market-bottom-arrives-this-week.html

financial crisis.⁵⁵ Some people made emotional decisions and paid dearly for it, missing out on a huge market recovery. Those who made more disciplined financial decisions were rewarded greatly for it.

That's why we say, when it comes to investing, it's more than just math. There's also a human component.

We understand we all go through cycles. Investors become greedier when others are greedy and become more afraid when others express fear.

In the best of all worlds, we would do just the opposite—when others in the market are being greedy, we try to discipline our clients to take their emotions out of investing. We don't want to be tied to any strategy. We want to invest for our clients based on the current economic environment.

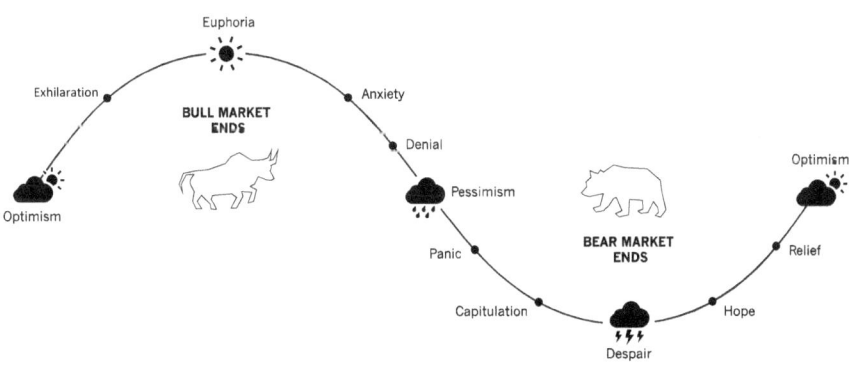

---

⁵⁵ T. Rowe Price Investor. 2018. "10 YEARS LATER." https://www.troweprice.com/content/dam/iinvestor/images/Pub_dwnld_Fall18Pubo9052018.pdf

Look at the chart above.[56] It's centered around a cycle of emotions. We all go through moments of excitement, thrills, and disappointment. This chart shows how you deal with a portfolio that is centered around the cycle of emotions rather than as based on numbers or analysis of your portfolio. Much of what we do as financial advisers is acting as a financial psychologist and helping to manage the emotions of our clients. Often, when emotions come into play, it is best to do nothing.

Your psyche can overpower rational thinking when you are under stress, and that stress can be induced by either panic or euphoria. Taking a rational and realistic approach to investing is essential.

We understand individual investors will likely be stressed when the market is down. Many have a low tolerance for risk, and their first emotional response is to move their assets to safer and more conservative investments. That is one of the reasons we ask clients in our first meeting about their level of risk tolerance. The last thing we want is for our clients to be making emotional decisions because of the markets.

Our role as financial advisers becomes key in situations like this. Some people need a partner to hold their hand and even talk them down when necessary, and at many times, we can be that partner.

Remember, times have changed. With twenty-four-hour business, news channels, and the internet, small investors have access to both the good news and the bad news instantly. They

---

[56] Searcy Financial. March 23, 2018. "Avoiding Emotional Investing." https://searcyfinancial.com/blog-posts/82-investments/161-avoiding-emotional-investing

also have access to commentary posing as news. As a result, they may jump into the market or into a stock at a less than ideal time.

The same is true of bad news when the market is down. You may prematurely cash out a position in a stock, or multiple positions in your portfolio, if you are allowing your emotions to govern your decisions.

Remember this: Emotional investing is synonymous with bad market timing.

Here is a tip for taking the emotions out of investing: Focus on the math. If it doesn't make sense to you, enlist your financial professional to help you work out the logic, the math, or the general reasoning on paper, free of the echo chamber of "what ifs" that may pervade your mind.

Let us explain further. Some people fall in love with a stock. They may buy it despite what the projections are, and they may hold onto it despite a precipitous decline. It is not hard to become emotionally attached to a stock in your portfolio if you have owned it a long time, and sometimes people even develop a fear of selling a particular stock. But, remember this piece of advice: You should not have feelings for a certain stock because it certainly has no feelings for you.

The best question to ask is this: If your assets were all in cash, would you still buy that stock? If the answer is "yes," that is a good thing. If the answer is "no," then it's clear you have an emotional attachment to that stock. You probably should not own that stock anymore. Find a way to remove yourself from that position in that stock.

Often, we see people who work for a publicly traded company become emotionally attached to that company's stock. We get it. You have a degree of pride for your company. You want to participate in that company's success. That makes sense. But you must make sure you don't get emotionally attached to that stock.

Keep in mind, the emotions of investing work both ways. When the market is going up, you can feel like you are missing out. You can become too optimistic and too aggressive when you don't need to be. But you can also become too pessimistic and too conservative. If the market is down, you may think you need to get out. It is our job as financial advisers to manage those emotions.

Taxes Are Inevitable

Some people also let their emotions get the better of them when it comes to taxes. They develop an emotional attachment to a stock and avoid selling it because they want to avoid taxes. You must understand taxes are inevitable. You are going to pay taxes eventually, whether you like it or not. Whether or not you could be in a lower tax bracket should be taken into consideration, though. Also, it would make sense to have a strategy in place—perhaps one of selling that stock over a period of years. But, trying to avoid taxes should never be the main reason you decide to hold onto a stock.

Conclusion

The concept of proper wealth management is to have a plan in place. You need to take a disciplined approach and remove all emotions so you can stick with the plan and stay the course.

Following a logical, repeatable process to develop a written plan that takes into account all aspects of your financial situation is key in helping you avoid situations where your emotions might affect your financial steering. Hopefully, you've seen through this book that, while there are a variety of asset types and strategies of differing levels of sophistication that can all be used in a portfolio, it's most important that they are coordinated in a simplified plan.

Taking the emotions out of investing, planning in reality and not based on optimism or pessimism, and avoiding the pitfalls of hasty decision-making are all powerful results of having a written plan to ensure all of your financial pieces are pulling in the same direction: yours.

Acknowledgments

While numerous people were invaluable in the creation of this book, we would like to recognize none more so than our families for supporting our vision of creating one of the best wealth management firms.

STEELPEAK WEALTH
Contact Us

If you would like to know more about SteelPeak Wealth and our process for building and maintaining wealth, we'd love to help. Please give us a call or visit us on the web:

(818) 835-8720

www.steelpeakwealth.com

www.ingramcontent.com/pod-product-compliance
Lightning Source LLC
Chambersburg PA
CBHW071418210526
45465CB00001B/439